THE WORLD SERIES

THE GREAT CONTESTS

BY
RICHARD J. BRENNER

EAST END PUBLISHING

With great love and affection to my children, Halle and Jason,
to my wife, Anita, and to my mother, Betty,
Thank you for your belief in me and your encouragement.
To Ms. Catherine Lynch, a rare teacher and spirit,
and to Malcolm Largman, another special teacher
and the first person who ever encouraged me to write—
to both of you, from a long time ago,
I've never forgotten either of you.

The author wishes to acknowledge the following:
The *New York Times*
Newsday
The World Series: A 75th Anniversary
edited by Joseph L. Reichler

Text Copyright © 1987; 1988; 1989; 1993; 1994 by Richard J. Brenner
Library of Congress Catalog Card Number: 87-15553
ISBN: 0-943403-22-7

—Cover Photo: R. Rahn

Library of Congress Cataloging-in-Publication Data
Brenner, Richard J., 1941–
   The World Series.

   Summary: Recounts memorable World Series contests,
including the 1955 series between the Brooklyn Dodgers and
the New York Yankees, the 1975 series between the
Cincinnati Reds and the Boston Red Sox, and the 1986
series between the New York Mets and the Boston Red Sox.
   1. World series (Baseball)—History—Juvenile
literature. [1. World series (Baseball) 2. Baseball—
History] I. Title.
GV863.A1B74   1987   796.357'782   87-15553
ISBN 0-943403-30-8

Printed in the United States of America.

This book is available at special quantity discounts for bulk
purchases for sales promotions, premiums, fund-raising or educa-
tional use.

For details write East End Publishing,
54 Alexander Dr., Syosset, New York 11791. (516) 364-6383

Contents

If you enjoy reading this book, you will want to see the back pages for instructions on how to order other exciting titles.

Introduction

The groundwork for what would come to be known as the World Series was laid in 1882 when Cincinnati, the top team in the American Association (the American League had not yet been formed), challenged Chicago of the National League to a championship series. But the players fought and argued so much that the teams just called it quits after they had played only a few games. From 1884–1890, the top teams in the two leagues played each other, but there were no set plans or number of games—one year they would play 3 games and another year, 15. Then they finally just stopped playing.

The first real World Series took place in 1903. It came about because the owner of the Pittsburgh Pirates, the National League champs, challenged the American League champs, the Boston Pilgrims (who would later be called the Red Sox), to a play-off series. The N.L. had been in existence for 28 years and wanted to put the upstart A.L., which was only three years old, in its place. But Boston, behind the pitching of Bill Dinneen (three victories, including two shutouts) and Cy Young (who would retire as the winningest pitcher in baseball with 511 victories), defeated the Pirates five games to three. (The leagues didn't finally settle on a best-of-seven format until 1922.)

The World Series wasn't played in 1904 because the owner and manager of the New York Giants refused to play a team from "the minor league". The outcry from fans was so strong, though, that the Series was resumed in 1905 and has been played every year since then.

The 1905 World Series was one of the most remarkable of all time. The Giants, who were again tops in the N.L., defeated the Philadelphia Athletics, 4-1. Each of the five victories were shutouts and three of the five were pitched by one man, Christy Mathewson! (Matty would go on to record 373 regular season wins and become one of the five original members of the Hall of Fame.)

In 1906, George Rohe helped the White Sox to one of the biggest upsets in a World Series. The White Sox, who hit so badly (their team average was a microscopic .230) that they were called the "hitless wonders", defeated the mighty Cubs, who had won 116 games during the season (still the record for most games won in a season), four games to two. George Rohe wasn't a very good ballplayer. He only played in the majors for three years (1905-1907) and only managed to hit .212, .258, and .213. And Rohe only got to play in the World Series because another player was injured. But for a brief, shining moment in time, George Rohe was a star as he batted .333 during the World Series. His triple in the first game led to a 2-1 victory and in game three, he hit another triple, which knocked in all the runs in a 3-0 win.

The Detroit Tigers, led by the great Ty Cobb, played in and lost the World Series in 1907, 1908, and 1909. Cobb is considered by many people to be the greatest player ever to wear spikes. He played in the majors for 24 seasons and, except for the first one, batted over .300 every year. He batted over .400 three times and when he retired, his career batting average was an astonishing .367, the highest career batting average of all time. But when it came to the World Series, Cobb managed to hit over .300 just once (in 1908), while batting .200 in 1907 and .231 in 1909.

Those first few contests show why the World Series has always delighted baseball fans: the clash of great teams; the thrill of watching the underdog upset the favorite; the drama of watching great stars shine (like Mathewson), or flicker (like Cobb); and the excitement of seeing little-known ballplayers with small talents (like George Rohe) briefly blaze like a shooting star across the baseball skies.

Through the years, the "Fall Classic" has provided millions of people the thrill of viewing this great sporting spectacle and sharing in its magic moments: watching Babe Ruth point to the centerfield seats in the 1932 Series and then, seeing him hit a home run right to where he had pointed; or watching Enos Slaughter race home from first base on a single to give the 1946 Cardinals the winning run in the seventh game. No one who saw the 1956 World Series will ever forget the fifth game when Yankee pitcher Don Larsen pitched the only perfect game in the history of the World Series. And no one who watched will ever forget the 1969 Series in which the "Miracle Mets", a team that had been picked for last place, beat the Baltimore Orioles.

Now we will take a close look at some of the most exciting World Series of all time—we hope that you enjoy the view.

CHAPTER 1

This Is Next Year!

In 1955, the world was, in many ways, not too different from the way it is today. Newspaper headlines, then and now, spoke about trouble in the Middle East, crime, and the need for nuclear disarmament.

In other ways, however, the world was very different from today. In the area of sports, for instance, the National Football League had only 12 teams, which were divided into Eastern and Western conferences. The AFC didn't exist and neither did the Super Bowl.

In baseball, the National and American leagues each had only eight teams, and the teams that were in first place at the end of the season played each other in the World Series. (Play-offs only happened on those rare occasions when two teams were tied at the end of the season.) Most regular-season games and all World Series games were played during the day and all the games were played on real grass; there wasn't any artificial turf.

For millions of people, though, the main way that the world is different now is that in 1955 the Dodgers played in Brooklyn, where they belonged, and not in Los Angeles.

Brooklyn is one of the five boroughs that make up the City of New York. Because it is so large and heavily populated, if Brooklyn had been a city, it would have been the fourth-largest city in America. But Brooklyn was divided up into neighborhoods—with names like Flatbush and Bensonhurst and Bay Ridge—that gave the people living in these areas the feeling that they were living in a small town.

The relationship between the people of Brooklyn and the Dodgers was a very special one that lasted through good times and bad times (as when the Dodgers finished in either sixth or seventh place 12 times in 17 seasons between 1922 and 1938). And even in the good times, there was always a letdown because the Dodgers were never able to win a World Series. Seven times they had tried and seven times they had lost. The last five times—1941, 1947, 1949, 1952, and 1953—they had lost to one team: the New York Yankees.

The Yankees were the undisputed lords of baseball. Their history rang with names like Babe Ruth, Lou Gehrig, and Joe DiMaggio. And between 1921, when they played in their first World Series, and 1953, 33 World Series had been played. Incredibly, the Yankees had played in 20 of them, winning 16 (6 of them in four-game sweeps)! Almost unbelievably, they had won 5 straight World Series between 1949 and 1953, and after a year's absence in 1954, they were hungry and back for more in 1955.

And what made all of this worse for Dodger fans was that the Yankees played just a subway ride away in the Bronx, another of New York City's boroughs. The Giants, the National League rivals of the Dodgers, played in the Polo Grounds, which was also just a subway ride from Ebbets Field, home of the Brooklyn Dodgers. So every year, Dodger fans had to suffer the taunts of people they worked with and went to school with. Sometimes a person even had Giant and Yankee fans in his own family!

But the Flatbush Faithful, as the Brooklyn fans were sometimes called, never lost their love or their faith in their team. And every year, the cry would ring out through the streets of Brooklyn from Coney Island to Bedford Avenue, "Wait until next year!"

Nineteen fifty-five looked as if it might really be "next year"—the year that Brooklyn finally won a World Series. They had gotten off to a great start by winning their first 10 games of the regular season and quickly building a big lead. They had finished a comfortable 13 1/2 games ahead of the second-place Milwaukee (now Atlanta) Braves.

They had an outstanding line-up that was anchored by future Hall-of-Famer Roy Campanella behind the plate. Campy, who was a great catcher, was also a ferocious hitter, who had hit .318 with 32 homers while driving in 107 runs during the regular season. He was also a team leader and one of the nicest men in the world. At first base was Gil Hodges, who hit 27 homers and had 102 RBI's. Many people consider him to be the finest fielding first baseman of all time. Second base was divided between Don Zimmer and Jim Gilliam, a switch-hitter. Shortstop belonged to Pee Wee Reese, the clutch-hitting, smooth-fielding captain of the Dodgers, who was also destined for the Hall of Fame. At third base was an exceptional man as well as an exceptional athlete—Jackie Robinson. Jackie, who had been an All-American running back in college and a star basketball player as well, was the first black man to be allowed to play in the major leagues. His ability, his character, and his courage set standards for everyone, both black and white. But he was nearly 37 years old now and time had robbed him of the skills that had earned him the Rookie of the Year Award in 1947 and the Most Valuable Player award in 1949. However, he still had his fierce pride and determination, and at critical times he could still win a ballgame with his bat, his glove, his legs, his head, or his courage. He also later earned election to the Hall of Fame.

Left field was shared by Gilliam—when he wasn't at second base—and a short, speedy Cuban named Sandy Amoros, who could hit for average and power. Center field was the property of another future Hall of Famer, Edwin "Duke" Snider. He was a spectacular fielder, had great speed, and was a super hitter. In 1955, he batted .309 while socking 42 homers and knocking in 136 runs. Right field was patrolled by Carl Furillo, an excellent outfielder with an exceptionally strong arm who had batted .314 with 26 homers and 95 RBI's.

The big question mark for the Dodgers was their pitching staff. Don Newcombe had gotten off to a fantastic start and had a 17-1 record in July. But he tailed off after that and was able to win only three games the rest of the season. Most of the other starting pitchers had also pitched poorly in the second half of the season. The Brooklyn front office turned to their minor leagues for help and came up with rookies Don Bessent and Roger Craig. Some of the Dodgers, like Johnny Podres, who had a 9-10 record, suffered from sore arms. Podres had also lost a decision to a metal batting cage near the end of the season and almost wasn't kept on the roster for the World Series. The only reliable exception to Brooklyn's pitching problems was Clem Labine, a tough right-hander with a wicked sinker who was used mostly as a relief pitcher.

The Yankees did not have it so easy in the American League. They were in a three-way fight for the pennant for most of the season with the Chicago White Sox and the Cleveland Indians. As late as September 13, the Yanks were two and one-half games back, but an eight-game winning streak put them into first place and they held on to win by a slim margin.

The Yankees also had a future Hall of Fame

catcher anchoring their team; his name was Lawrence "Yogi" Berra. He had hit .272 with 27 homers and 108 RBI's, and acted as a coach on the field for the Yankees. The Yankees used a platoon system at first base with lefty Joe Collins playing against right-handed pitching and righty Bill "Moose" Skowron playing against left-handed pitchers. Together they had combined for 25 home runs and 106 RBI's. The second baseman was Billy Martin, the hero of the Yanks' 1953 World Series victory over the Dodgers. Martin would go on to become manager of the Yankees, and other teams, too. Shortstop was shared by Phil Rizzuto and Jerry Coleman—terrific fielders and adequate hitters. Third base was handled by the steady Gil McDougald.

The outfield was solid with Irv Noren in left, the great Mickey Mantle in center, and the clutch-hitting, hard-throwing Hank Bauer in right. Mantle had had an outstanding season with a .309 average, 37 homers, 99 RBI's, but he had torn a muscle in his thigh two weeks before the Series was to begin and it was uncertain if he could play. The Yankees had strong reserves but all of them put together wouldn't make up for the absence of Mantle. The Yankees had a solid pitching staff led by Whitey Ford, Tommy Byrne, and Bob Turley. The manager of the Yankees was Casey Stengel, the man whom many people consider to be the greatest manager of all time. Even if Mantle couldn't play, most experts figured that either Stengel would find a way for the Yankees to win or

Brooklyn would find a way to lose.

The weather was overcast the morning of the first game, and although the sky cleared before noon, the 63,000 fans who filled Yankee Stadium saw the Yanks drop a little more rain on Dodger dreams.

The Dodgers did manage to jump out to an early lead against Yankee ace Whitey Ford in the second inning, as Carl Furillo hit a midget home run to right field that just hit the top of the low railing and bounced into the seats. Jackie Robinson followed with a tremendous drive to left center that measured more than 400 feet and he raced to third with a triple. Don Zimmer blooped a single over the infield and the Dodgers led, 2-0.

But the Yankees, like some jealous Greek gods, tied the game in the bottom of the inning on a two-run home run off Don Newcombe by rookie left fielder Elston Howard. Howard, who was playing while Mantle continued to nurse his injury, became one of the few players to hit a home run in his first at-bat in a World Series.

The Dodgers took the lead again in the top of the third when Duke Snider hit a tremendous blast into the right-field stands. But the Yanks tied it in their next turn at bat on a walk, a single, and two groundouts. In the fourth, Joe Collins hit a homer to give the Yanks a 4-3 lead, and in the sixth, he followed a single by Yogi Berra with another homer and the Yanks led, 6-3. One out later, Billy Martin lined a triple over Gilliam's head in left field and Walter Alston, the

Dodger manager, decided that Newcombe had pitched long enough. He brought in Don Bessent, a rookie right-hander and Casey Stengel responded by putting in a left-handed pinch hitter, Eddie Robinson, for Rizzuto. But Robinson never got to swing the bat because after he took a pitch for a ball and Bessent went into his windup for the next pitch, Martin took off in an attempt to steal home. Martin and the pitch arrived at almost the same instant but a quick tag by Campy was just in time to get Martin and retire the Yanks.

Furillo opened the eighth inning with a single for his third straight hit. Hodges flied out and Jackie Robinson hit a sharp grounder to third base for what should have been an easy out, maybe a double play, but Gil McDougald let the ball get by him and Furillo made it to third and Robinson to second. Zimmer then hit a sacrifice fly that scored Furillo and sent Robinson to third. Ford checked Robinson, who was dancing off third. As Whitey went into his windup, Jackie dashed for home. Ford delivered the pitch and Yogi made the tag, but this time the umpire yelled "safe". Berra argued the call but, as always, the umpire won the argument. It was the 18th time that Jackie had stolen home in his remarkable career, and only the 9th time that it had ever been accomplished in a World Series game. The Yanks' lead had been cut to 6-5.

The Dodgers came close in the ninth when, after Snider singled, Campy hit a wicked liner to deep right field. But it didn't have enough height and the Yanks won the opening game.

Although Mantle's injury didn't allow him to play, Joe Collins, who had hit two homers, told reporters that Mickey had helped the Yanks win. How? Because he had used Mickey's bat to swat the homers. "I'm going to keep right on using it. There's real good wood in that bat."

Walt Alston, the Dodger manager, assured everyone that the team was still confident and so was he. Campy, who always seemed to be able to manage a smile and find a silver lining behind any dark cloud, spoke about his long out in the ninth. "If I had just hit it a little higher instead of on a line, it would have been in the stands."

For the Brooklyn Dodgers, there always seemed to be an "if".

The Dodgers looked sharp in the beginning of the second game. Billy Loes shut the Yanks out for three innings and struck out five. He was especially tough in the second when, after Yogi had reached second, he struck out Collins, Howard, and Martin. And the Dodgers broke through for a run off Tommy Byrne in the fourth when Reese doubled and Snider singled him home.

The Yanks answered back in the bottom of the fourth when, with two out, Berra singled and Collins walked. Elston Howard singled for one run and Martin singled for a second. Eddie Robinson, pinch hitting for Rizzuto, was hit by a pitch and Tommy Byrne, the Yankee pitcher, hit a two-run single. The Dodgers managed to hold the Yanks the rest of the way and come up with a run in the fifth, but it was too late. Tommy Byrne pitched a five-hitter and the Yanks had won again, 4-2.

The victory was especially sweet for the 35-year-old Tommy Bryne because he had had to work hard and struggle his way back to the majors after spending a year in the minors learning how to become an effective pitcher.

The Dodgers had battered southpaws (left-handers) all year. In fact, only one left-hander had pitched a complete game against them and he had lost. Now within 24 hours, they had lost to two lefties and had managed, naturally, to do it in the World Series.

After the game, Pee Wee Reese, talking about Billy Loes, said, "The way he was going, I thought he would shut them out. I thought this was going to be Billy's day."

But it wasn't Billy's day and it wasn't the Dodger's day. They were down two games to none and no team had ever been down 2-0 in a 4-of-7 Series and come back to win it!

For the third game, the scene shifted to cozy Ebbets Field, the home of the Brooklyn Dodgers. "Bullet" Bob Turley, a fast-balling right-hander who had had a 17-13 record, opened for the Yankees. To the delight of the Flatbush Faithful, the Dodgers jumped out to a 2-0 lead in the first when Campy smacked a two-out homer after Pee Wee had walked.

But the Yanks went on the attack in the second as Mantle, despite the fact he was playing in pain, smashed a homer into the center-field stands off Dodger starter Johnny Podres. Bill "Moose" Skowron, playing first base against the left-handed Podres, doubled to left. Podres retired the next two hitters, but Rizzuto singled to left. Skowron was running all the way with two out but a fine throw by Sandy Amoros got the ball to Campy in plenty of time. But Skowron, who had played college football at Purdue, barreled into Campy and the sure-handed catcher dropped the ball as Skowron scored the tying run. The Dodgers had lost the lead again; they could not afford to lose another game.

Brooklyn responded by bouncing back in their half of the second. Robinson singled, Amoros walked, and Podres bunted so well while attempting to sacrifice that he beat the throw. Turley walked Gilliam to force in a run and Casey Stengel walked out to the mound to remove Turley. Tom Morgan, the new pitcher, walked Pee Wee to force in another run before retiring the side. Brooklyn upped their lead to 6-2 in the fourth as Gilliam singled, Duke walked, Campy singled in Gilliam—moving Duke to third—and Furillo hit a long foul fly to left, allowing Duke to tag up and score.

The Yanks threatened in the sixth when Mantle came up to hit after McDougald and Berra had singled. The Flatbush Faithful grew tense but Podres got Mantle to ground into a double play. The Yanks scored their last run of the day on a walk to Rizzuto and a pinch triple by Andy Carey. But the Dodgers answered with two more runs in the bottom of the seventh, which was started off by some great base running by Jackie Robinson. He lined a ball into the left-field corner and cruised around second base. Elston Howard wound up to fire the ball into second and as soon as he did, Jackie put on the afterburners and slid into third.

The Dodgers, with their 8-3 victory, had cut the Yanks' lead to 2-1 and Johnny Podres, who turned 23 that day, laughed, "This was the best birthday present I ever had."

In game four, the Yanks jumped out to a quick lead on a Gil McDougald homer off Carl Erskine in the first inning. They added another run in the second on an RBI single by Rizzuto. The Dodgers cut the lead to 2-1 on a single by Amoros and a two-bagger by Gilliam but the Yanks upped it to 3-1 on an RBI single by Billy Martin in the top of the fourth.

In the bottom of the fourth, the Brooklyn bats began to boom. Campy homered to left off Don Larsen, and after Furillo beat out an infield roller, Gil Hodges hit a huge homer over the scoreboard in right center to give the Dodgers a 4-3 lead.

The crowd in Ebbets Field was roaring, and the roars grew louder when Clem Labine, the Dodgers' relief ace, came in to snuff out a fifth-inning threat. In the bottom of the fifth, Larsen walked Gilliam, and after he threw two balls to Pee Wee, Stengel replaced him with Johnny Kucks. Pee Wee beat out an infield bouncer after Gilliam had stole second. Duke Snider strolled to the plate, jumped on a pitch, and sent it sailing high and far over the right-field screen and across Bedford Avenue to give the Dodgers a 7-3 lead. The fans went wild!

But they grew hushed in the sixth when the Yanks pushed across two quick runs as Howard singled, Martin doubled him home, and pinch hitter Eddie Robinson doubled home Martin. Only a great catch by Snider in center field prevented more scoring.

The Dodgers, though, picked up another run in the seventh and Labine pitched no-hit ball for the final three innings, so the Dodgers won 8-5 and evened the series at 2-2. They had climbed up and out of the hole they had been in but they hadn't impressed the Yanks. Berra said that Labine had been "lucky" and Phil "The Scooter" Rizzuto said, "We'll win the Series. Maybe it will go seven games, but we'll win it."

But Brooklyn had other ideas. In the second inning of game five, after Hodges singled, Amoros drilled a homer over the screen in right off Bob Grim. In the third, Snider continued to punish Yankee pitching with a solo blast over the screen, and the Dodgers led 3-0 behind rookie Roger Craig's pitching. They might have gotten more, too, but Irv Noren, playing center for Mantle (who had aggravated his injury) made an excellent catch. The Yanks did break through with a run in the fourth though when the pesky Martin singled in Berra. The Dodgers scored again in the fifth with a towering home run way over the screen in right by—who else?—Duke Snider. It was his fourth homer of the series and he became the only player ever to hit four home runs in more than one World Series (he had also done it in 1952).

The Yanks stormed back with a solo homer by pinch hitter Bob Cerv in the seventh off Roger Craig and another by Yogi in the eighth off Clem Labine. Labine avoided more trouble by getting Martin to ground into a double play. After an RBI single by Jackie Robinson in the bottom of the eighth, Labine knocked off the Yanks one-two-three in the ninth for a 5-3 Brooklyn win, and the Dodgers led the Series, 3-2.

In the clubhouse after the game, an excited Jackie Robinson was shouting happily "Four straight, four straight." And, even the usually quiet Gil Hodges told reporters, "If you think we went after them at Ebbets Field, wait until tomorrow at the Stadium. We'll swarm all over them like a pack of tigers."

But it was the Yankees who wound up devouring the Dodgers. The Yankees scored five runs in the first inning off lefty Karl Spooner, helped by two fielding mistakes by Gilliam, and a three-run homer by Moose Skowron that just made it into the lower right-field stands. And in the third, Snider injured his knee and had to leave the game when he stepped into a hole while chasing a fly ball. No one knew if he would be ready for game seven if the Dodgers lost game six.

The Dodgers scored a meaningless run in the fourth and mounted a couple of threats later in the game but they were turned back by the pitching of

Whitey Ford (who gave up only four hits while striking out eight for his second victory in the Series) and a marvelous fielding play in the seventh inning by Joe Collins, who had replaced Skowron at first base in the fifth.

Casey Stengel and the Yankee players were confident about the seventh game. Tommy Byrne, who had baffled the Dodgers in the second game, was all ready, and after all, the Yankees almost always won and the Dodgers never had.

The weather was sunny on Tuesday, October 4, as 62,455 people filled Yankee Stadium for the seventh and final game. Baseball fans all across the city huddled around TV sets or turned on their radios. People who had to go out walked through the streets with portable radios close to their ears. Snider could play, but Jackie Robinson was out with an injured foot. The umpire yelled, "Play ball." The game began.

Although the Yankees threatened in the second and third, the game remained scoreless until the fourth inning when Campy doubled to left and Gil Hodges brought him home with a two-out single off Byrne. Berra doubled to lead off the Yankee fourth but Podres retired the next three batters as the tension mounted. The Dodgers eked out another run in the sixth when Pee Wee, who had begun the inning with a single, eventually came in to score on a sacrifice fly by Hodges off Bob Grim who had relieved Byrne. The last out of the inning was made by George Shuba, who pinch-hit for Don Zimmer. That meant that Gilliam would move to second base and Sandy Amoros would come in to play left field.

Podres began the bottom of the sixth by walking Martin, and McDougald followed with a bunt single. The next batter was Yogi Berra, the Yankee clean-up hitter. One swing and the Dodgers' dream could be demolished. The Dodgers' outfield played Yogi deep and around to right to guard against his left-hand power.

Podres checked the runners and delivered a pitch on the outside part of the plate. Yogi swung and hit a fly ball down the left-field line. He hadn't pulled the ball, he had hit it to the opposite field, and Amoros was way out of position. As Sandy desperately raced across the outfield grass, Martin headed for third and McDougald rounded second. As the ball came out of the blue sky, Sandy, still running at full speed, stuck out his glove as far as he could and caught the ball! Then in one motion, he turned and fired the ball to Pee Wee, who relayed it to Hodges at first to double up McDougald. Amoros, who had just entered the game, had taken a game-tying hit away from Berra and turned it into a double play!

In the eighth, the Yanks erupted again when Rizzuto and McDougald singled. But Podres got Berra on a shallow fly to right and fanned the dangerous Hank Bauer.

All across the city, people stopped what they were doing to watch or listen to whether the Dodgers could hold their 2-0 lead in the ninth inning. Dodger fans, used to sudden disaster, held their breath. Skowron grounded to Podres for the first out and Cerv flied to left for the second out. Elston Howard came up to hit and time seemed to stop as Podres looked in for the sign and then the pitch was there and Howard hit a routine grounder to short. Pee Wee picked it up and threw it to Hodges at first for the final out of the 1955 World Series.

On the field, the Dodgers jumped and yelled for joy while all across Brooklyn, the noise of thousands of celebrating fans filled the air. People came out into the streets to shout their joy and share it with friends, neighbors, and total strangers. Pots were banged and caravans of cars with horns blasting moved along Flatbush Avenue and Ocean Parkway to announce that the wait was over.

NEXT YEAR WAS NOW!

CHAPTER 2

A Long Time Coming

The Pittsburgh Pirates and Cincinnati Reds were the dominant teams in the National League. The Pirates were about to represent the Eastern Division for the fifth time since 1970, while the Reds would be representing the Western Division for the fourth time since 1970.

The Pirates were out for revenge because they had lost to the Reds in the play-offs in 1970 and 1972. The Reds were on a mission of their own. They wanted to do what the Pirates had done in 1971. They wanted to win the 1975 World Series.

The Pirates had taken the Eastern Division by a six-and-one-half-game margin over the Phillies, mainly on the hitting of a group of sluggers led by Dave Parker with a .305 average, 25 homers, and 101 RBI's. He had plenty of support, too, from players like Willie Stargell (.292, 22, 90); Al Oliver (.280, 18,84); Richie Zisk (.290, 20, 75); Rennie Stennett, a hard-hitting second baseman (during the season, he became only the second player in baseball history to get seven hits in a game); and Manny Sanguillen, an excellent defensive catcher who also managed to hit .328.

The Reds started slowly during the regular season, but after manager Sparky Anderson moved all-star Pete Rose from left field to third base to make room in the line-up for George Foster's big bat, "the Big Red Machine" went into overdrive and won the Western Division title by a whopping 20 games. In one awesome stretch, they won 41 of 50 games!

The Reds seemed to have an all-star at every position, starting with Pete Rose, who had hit .317, marking the 10th time in 11 years that he had hit .300 or better. Behind the plate was the great Johnny Bench, the best catcher in baseball, who had hit .283 while smacking 28 homers and driving in 110 runs. At first base was Tony Perez (.282, 20, 109); Foster added punch in left with a .300 average and 23 homers; and Ken Griffey in right had hit .305. Dave Concepcion at short and Cesar Geronimo in center provided spectacular defense and respectable offense. The player who provided the spark that revved up the engine of the Big Red Machine, however, was second baseman Joe Morgan. At 5'7" and 155 pounds, Joe was small in size but large in ability. He had led the Reds in hitting with a .327 average while hitting 17 homers, driving in 94 runs, and scoring 107 himself. He also stole 68 bases in 78 attempts.

The Reds also had a solid group of starting pitchers headed by lefty Don Gullet, who had a 15-4 record and a 2.42 ERA, despite missing two months with a broken thumb. Right-handers Jack Billingham and Gary Nolan had also won 15 games and lefty Fred Norman had a 12-4 record. The bullpen was anchored by Rawly Eastwick (22 saves, 2.60 ERA); Will McEnany (15 saves, 2.47 ERA); Clay Carroll; and Pedro Borbon. The Machine was oiled and gassed and ready to run.

Pittsburgh manager Danny Murtagh started his ace, Jerry Reuss, in the first game of the best-of-five series. Reuss had an 18-11 regular-season record with a 2.54 ERA and had beaten the Reds three times. Murtagh had decided to feed the Reds a steady diet of left-handers since they had shown weakness against southpaws with a regular-season record of only 26-22. The Pirates jumped out to an early 2-0 lead at Cincinnati's Riverfront Stadium but the Reds cut it to 2-1 on an RBI single by pitcher Don Gullett. Joe Morgan began a three-run Reds' rally in the third when he drew a base on balls and then swiped second and third base on consecutive pitches. Reuss, losing his concentration because of Morgan's antics, walked Bench, and Perez followed with a single to score Morgan. Griffey then hit a two-out double to score Bench and Perez. They wrapped up the game in the fifth with four more runs, the last two coming on Gullett's first major-league home run, and cruised to an 8-3 victory.

In game two, the Reds got all the runs they needed in the first inning off lefty Jim Rooker when Rose singled and Perez homered. The Reds ran wild on the bases, stealing an almost unbelievable seven bases (in seven tries!), led by Ken Griffey with three. Norman and Eastwick combined on a five-hitter as the Reds romped, 6-1.

As the "scene of the crime" shifted to Pittsburgh's Three Rivers Stadium for game three, Sparky Anderson reminded the Reds, "You've got to win three games, not just two. We've been annihilated by Pittsburgh before and they could take three in a row."

Rookie John Candelaria was pitching a spectacular game for the Pirates. He had struck out seven of the first nine Reds and had given up only one hit, a second-inning homer by Dave Concepcion. He held a 2-1 lead entering the eighth inning, though, thanks to a two-run homer by Al Oliver in the sixth. "Candy" struck out the first two batters in the eighth—Griffey and Cesar Geronimo—for his 13th and 14th strikeouts, which broke the play-off record of 13 that Tom Seaver had set against the Reds in 1973. But pinch-hitter Merv Rettenmund walked and then Pete Rose got the second hit off Candy, a towering home run over the left-field fence that gave the Reds a 3-2 lead.

The Pirates caught up in the ninth with two walks after two singles forced in a run. But the Reds scored two in the tenth, beginning with a surprise two-strike bunt by Griffey and ending with a double by Joe Morgan. Pedro Borbon retired the Pirates in order in the bottom of the tenth and the Big Red Machine was humming and on its way to the World Series.

The Oakland A's had been ruling supreme over

the Kingdom of Baseball. They had won five straight divisional titles and for the last three years, they had won the World Series. And now they were ready for more; they were ready for number four.

The A's had two top starting pitchers, southpaws Vida Blue (22-11) and Ken Holtzman (18-14). They had an excellent bullpen led by Rollie Fingers (24 saves and 10 wins) and supported by Paul Lindblad (9-1) and rookie Jim Todd (8-3).

They were solid on defense and had a strong offense led by left fielder Claudell Washington, first baseman Joe Rudi, and "Mr. October" himself, Reggie Jackson. (Reggie is called Mr. October because of his excellent performance during the month of October, the month of play-off and World Series games). During the season, he had tied for the league lead with 36 homers.

The A's had taken an early lead in their division and, after April 28, had held first place for all but two days. They wound up coasting in to a seven-game lead over second-place Kansas City and they had such an easy time and played with such confidence that Reggie said, "We only played five games where we were nervous and excited and afraid to lose: three against K.C. when they made a move at the A's in September; a game against the White Sox that clinched first place; and a late-season game against the Boston Red Sox to "psych" Boston out in case they met in the play-offs." They won all five games.

The Red Sox, always known for their hitting, had

led the majors with a .275 average, and led the A.L. with 756 RBI's while swatting 134 home runs.

They had beaten Baltimore out for first place in the East, led by Fred Lynn and Jim Rice, two of the best rookies ever to come to one team at the same time. Leftfielder Rice had hit .309 with 22 homers and 102 RBI's, while center fielder Lynn had hit .331 with 21 homers and 105 RBI's. Dwight Evans, one of the best defensive players in baseball, completed the outfield.

The infield had been anchored by veteran Carl Yastrzemski at first base. Yaz, who had been one of the best players in baseball in his 15 years with Boston, had injured his shoulder during the season and only batted .269. But despite his 36 years, when the team was in a tight spot, he would usually find a way to win. Because Rice had broken his hand the last week of the season, Yaz had to move back to left field, where he had played for 14 years, and Cecil Cooper, who had hit .311 as the designated hitter, replaced Yaz at first. Second baseman Danny Doyle, who hit .298, provided a solid double-play combination with shortstop Rick Burleson; Rico Petrocelli at third completed the infield. Carlton Fisk provided defense behind the plate and a big bat as shown by his .331 regular-season average. They also had good bench strength in Juan Beniquez and the powerful Bernie Carbo. Their pitching staff was led by starters Luis Tiant (18-14), Rick Wise (19-12), and Bill Lee (17-9), while Roger Moret and Dick Drago were the main men in the bullpen.

If the Sox needed inspiration, Reggie Jackson

may have provided it when he said that he would rather play Boston than Baltimore because the Orioles were used to play-off pressure. "That," said Reggie, "should give us an edge. You can read about it and hear about it, but until you're there you don't know what the pressure is like."

When the game started, though, it was the A's who seemed to feel the pressure as they gave the Sox two runs with the help of three errors. In the seventh, they made another error and added in some sloppy playing and Boston came up with five more runs.

After the game, Reggie said, "It looks like the Jolly Green Giant (Oakland wears green uniforms) was cut down to size. That's the way the Sox are supposed to play." The Sox actually had done their part by committing three errors, which set a play-off record of seven errors in one game. But the three-hit pitching of Luis Tiant had kept the A's bats quiet and Boston beat them 7-1.

But the A's had lost the first game of the play-offs to Baltimore in each of the last two years and had gone on to win, and they were confident of beating Boston. Reggie improved their confidence by hitting a two-run homer in the first and they added another run for a 3-0 lead. Yaz hit a two-run homer and the Sox scored another run to tie the game 3-3 in the fourth. In the sixth, Yaz doubled and scored the winning run off Rollie Fingers, who had had a 3-0 record against Boston during the season. Petrocelli poled a solo homer in the seventh and Lynn added another to complete a 6-3 Boston victory.

After the game, talking about Yaz's hitting and the two great throws that he had made, Reggie said, "Yaz brought them back. All their players hung in there, but Yaz brought them back."

The A's had almost always played their best under pressure as in the 1973 World Series when they had been down three games to two against the Mets and then had come back to beat Tom Seaver in the sixth game and had gone on to take the Series.

But Boston took an early 1-0 lead on an unearned run and added three more in the fifth on three singles, a double by Yaz, and a wild pitch. The A's finally scored one run in the sixth but Boston got another in the top of the eighth. In the bottom of the eighth, the A's made their move. They had one run in and runners on first and second with Reggie at the plate. Reggie lined the ball toward the alley in left center for what looked like a sure triple. But Yaz dove full length at the ball and held Jackson to a single as only one run scored. Dick Drago came in and got Joe Rudi to ground into a double play to end the inning and then shut them down in the ninth.

The Red Sox had dethroned the A's as champions and won the A.L. pennant.

The 72nd World Series was scheduled to begin in Boston's Fenway Park. Fenway, built in 1912, is a very special place in which to play or watch a baseball game. Unlike today's modern stadiums, which are large and all shaped about the same, Fenway Park is small, with a seating capacity of only 32,583, so most fans can be very close to the field. Fenway Park also has a lot of little nooks and oddities that make it a difficult park to play in, especially if you are unfamiliar with it. The most memorable feature in Fenway is the left-field wall, which is known as "The Wall" or, because of the difficulties it presents and the color it is painted, "The Green Monster". The Wall is close to home plate and it is high—37 feet high with a 23-foot screen on top of it.

It is difficult to pitch at Fenway because The Wall is only 315 feet from home plate, which is a short distance for major-league hitters. It presents difficulties on defense, especially to left fielders because, as Gene Mauch, the manager of the Angels, put it, "The ball can bounce off The Wall and go anywhere." And the Green Monster can hurt hitters as well. As Ted Kluszewski, a Cincinnati coach and former major leaguer, puts it, "You see The Wall for the first time and you want to really go for it. But that can mess up your swing."

Boston would have a definite advantage when the games were played at Fenway, but when they moved to Cincinnati, the Red Sox would have to be concerned with the artificial turf at Riverfront Stadium. A ball hit on the turf moves much more quickly than a ball hit on natural grass and that means that it gets to the fielder more quickly. Routine grounders can easily become singles and singles can quickly become doubles or triples.

It promised to be a very exciting series, and no matter which team won, the winning team and city would be v-e-r-y happy. Cincinnati hadn't won a World Series in 35 years and Boston hadn't won in 57 years. Both cities had waited a long time and both teams were thirsty for the taste of victory.

Don Gullett, the starter for the Reds in the first game, told reporters, "I'm not concerned with The Monster. My hard stuff will get the job done."

Gullett and Boston starter Luis Tiant hooked up in a pitching duel and neither team scored for six innings. Both teams mounted threats but clutch pitching and super defense kept the game scoreless. Both Geronimo and Concepcion threw Boston batters out at home plate.

But in the seventh inning, it all began to fall apart for Gullett and the Reds when Tiant singled for his first hit in three years. Next, Gullett fielded a bunt by Evans and while he was throwing to second, he slipped and the ball wound up in center field. Doyle then singled to load the bases and Yaz singled to score Tiant. By the time the inning was over, the Sox had six runs. That was more than enough support for Tiant, who stalled the Big Red Machine by tossing a five-hit shutout against them.

In the second game, Boston scored in the first inning on some odd plays. It began when Foster misplayed a Cecil Cooper line drive into a double. Doyle then beat out an infield single as Cooper went to third. Yaz bounced back to the pitcher, Jack Billingham, who forced Doyle at second, while Cooper tried to score. But Concepcion threw home and Cooper was tagged out in a run-down while Yaz ran to second. The Red Sox finally scored when Fisk singled Yaz home.

The Reds tied it in the fourth, but Boston went ahead 2-1 in the sixth when Yaz and Petrocelli sandwiched singles around an error by Concepcion. Bill Lee took the one-run lead and a four-hitter into the ninth inning, but Bench, looking for an outside pitch, guessed correctly and lined it into right for a double. Dick Drago, who had saved two play-offs games, was brought in to face Perez. Perez grounded out as Bench took third. Foster came to the plate hoping to make up for his fielding mistake in the first inning, but he hit a shallow fly to left and Bench had to hold at third. The Reds were down to their last out as Concepcion prepared to bat. He wanted to make up for his sixth-inning error and he didn't want to make the last out of the game as he had in the first game. "It's not going to happen again," he told himself. It didn't. He hit a high bouncer up the middle for an infield single as Bench scored the tying run. Concepcion then stole second on a very close play and rode home on a double to left center by Ken Griffey. The Reds had come back with two runs in the ninth to take a 3-2 lead. Rawly Eastwick, who had shut the Sox out in the eighth inning, repeated his performance in the ninth and Cincinnati had evened the Series at 1-1.

The Series shifted to Riverfront Stadium for the third game, with Gary Nolan pitching for the Reds and Rick Wise for Boston.

Carlton Fisk opened the scoring for Boston with a home run in the second inning, the first home run by either team in the Series. In the fourth, Perez walked and then surprised everyone by stealing second. He had stolen only one base the entire season. But he could have saved his energy because Bench followed with a home run and the Reds led, 2-1. Concepcion and Geronimo, who together had hit only 11 homers all season long, hit back-to-back homers in the fifth. And after Rose tripled over Lynn's head later in the inning, Jim Burton, a left-hander, was brought in to pitch to Griffey and Morgan, both of whom are left-handed hitters. But Burton walked Griffey (who then stole second) and Morgan hit a sacrifice fly that scored Rose. The Reds led, 5-1, and were feeling pretty good.

Boston scored a run in the sixth off Gary Darcy (Nolan had left the game with a stiff neck) on two walks, a wild pitch, and a sacrifice fly by Lynn. In the seventh, Bernie Carbo, who had started out in the majors with Cincinnati, hit a pinch homer to cut the Reds' lead to 5-3. In the ninth, Dwight Evans hit a two-run homer and Boston had come back to tie the game! Now the Reds were feeling pretty lame.

Geronimo began the tenth inning with a walk and George Armbrister was sent up to bunt him to second. What happened next caused a commotion that still excites baseball fans in Boston. Armbrister bunted, Carlton Fisk pounced on it, and threw toward second. Because Armbrister didn't move, he and Fisk collided and the throw went into center field. Fisk argued—and many experts agreed—that Armbrister should have been called out for interference. The umpires disagreed and the Reds wound up with runners at second and third. Southpaw Roger Moret was brought in to walk Rose intentionally (which would load the bases to set up a force play at home) and to pitch to the next two batters, who were left-handed. Anderson crossed up the strategy by sending up Rettenmund, a righty, to hit for Griffey, but Moret fanned him anyway for the first out. Joe Morgan came up next and smacked a tremendous drive to left center and Geronimo trotted home with the winning run. So much for strategy. The Reds were feeling *very* good!

Neither team had hit a homer in cozy Fenway Park, but in spacious Riverfront Stadium, they tied a Series record by hammering out six of them. Baseball can be a funny game.

The Reds began romping in the very first inning of game four off Luis Tiant, who had shut them out in the first game. Rose started it with a single and came home to score on a double by Griffey. A strong relay by Burleson caught Griffey at third when he tried to stretch the hit into a triple. Morgan, though, followed with a walk and Bench doubled him home for a 2-0 lead.

Reds pitcher Fred Norman cruised along for three

innings but in the fourth, the roof caved in. First Fisk singled to left and Lynn singled to right. After an out, Evans tripled home both runners to tie the game. Burleson knocked in Evans with what should have been a single, but alert and aggressive base running stretched it into a double. Borbon came in and Tiant greeted him with a single—his second hit in three years—and Burleson took third. Perez then bobbled Beniquez's grounder and Burleson scored while Tiant moved to second. Yaz delivered a two-out single and Tiant scored the fifth run of the inning.

Before Boston had a chance to feel too good about their 5-2 lead, the Reds, with the help of poor Sox fielding, bounced back with two runs in the bottom of the inning. Foster singled with two out and moved to second on an error. Concepcion hit a blooper to left center that fell between three Boston players for a double while Foster scored. Geronimo then hit a ball that bounced in front of Beniquez in left and then over his head for a triple as Concepcion scored.

The score was still 5-4 in favor of Boston as the Reds came to bat in the bottom of the ninth. Geronimo led with a single and was bunted to second. Rose walked and Griffey hit a drive deep to center where Lynn made a spectacular, over-the-shoulder catch while running at full speed. There were two outs now and Joe Morgan was up with a chance to win the game. But little Joe wouldn't be the hero today. Tiant got him to pop up to Yaz for his second victory. The Series was tied, 2-2.

Boston scored in the opening inning of game five on a triple by Doyle and a sacrifice fly by Yaz. The Reds threatened in their turn at bat but Beniquez threw Rose out at home. They tied it in the fourth, though, when Perez broke out of an 0-15 slump with a home run; and they made it 2-1 in the fifth when Gullett singled with two out and Rose doubled him home. In the sixth inning, Morgan walked and scooted to third on a hit-and-run single by Bench. Three pitches later, Perez poled his second homer of the game and the Reds led, 5-1.

The Reds scored another run in the eighth and Gullett, who was pitching a two-hitter, took a 6-1 lead into the ninth. He retired the first two batters, but then Yaz and Fisk singled and Lynn doubled Yaz home. Rawly Eastwick, who had won games two and three in relief, came in to save the game for Gullett by getting Petrocelli with a strike-out on three straight pitches. The Reds needed one more win.

The teams returned to Boston for game six, which turned out to be one of the most exciting games in World Series history. For many people, especially Bostonians, it became known simply as THE GAME.

Boston had to win to force a seventh game and they struck early. In the first inning, Yaz and Fisk each rapped two-out singles. Fred Lynn, who had not hit much during the Series, came up and hit the ball long and high and over the Boston bullpen in right center for a three-run homer. The fans in Fenway loved it.

The Reds, though, evened matters in the fifth

when a walk, a Pete Rose single, and a long triple off the center-field wall by Griffey produced two runs, and a Johnny Bench single off The Wall in left scored Griffey.

Griffey and Morgan both singled to left to start the seventh but Tiant got Bench and Perez to fly out. George Foster, though, came through with a 400-foot blast for a double and both runners scored. Geronimo hit a homer in the eighth to make it 6-3 and the Reds were ready to celebrate. As Tiant was taken out of the game, he felt gloomy despite the standing ovation that he received from the Boston fans.

The Sox were down to their last six outs as Lynn opened the eighth with a single. Petrocelli walked but then Rawly Eastwick came in and retired the next two batters. Bernie Carbo came up now to pinch-hit against the team that had traded him. In game two, Eastwick had fanned him. This time, as the crowd sat tense, the count went to three-and-two. Eastwick delivered, Carbo swung, and the ball rocketed into the center-field bleachers for a three-run homer. The Fenway fans went wild; the game was tied, 6-6.

In the ninth inning, the Sox loaded the bases with nobody out and Lynn came up to bat. He only managed to lift a short fly to left and when Doyle tried to tag up, Foster threw him out. Petrocelli made the third out and Boston had wasted a golden opportunity. So now they were going to extra innings.

In the 11th, Rose led off by being hit with a pitch. Griffey tried to bunt him into scoring position but Fisk pounced on the ball and forced Rose at second. Morgan came up and smacked a long fly to right field. Evans raced back as the ball headed for the stands, and at the last second, he leaped up and made a spectacular, one-handed catch to rob Morgan of a home run. Then he threw the ball into the infield and Griffey, who was already at third, was doubled up. In the wink of an eye, a game that looked to be lost was saved, for now anyway.

Bench led off the 12th by hitting a high pop foul on which Fisk made a remarkable catch while leaning into the stands. Perez and Foster singled out but Rick Wise got Concepcion on a fly and fanned Geronimo.

Carlton Fisk led off the bottom of the 12th by hitting the first pitch deep down the left-field line. If it stayed fair, it was gone. As Fisk saw the ball sail toward the seats, it began to hook. As he watched the ball come down, he twisted his body as though he could will it to stay fair. And then it landed high up against the foul pole; it was a home run. Boston had won 7-6; the Series was all even. Carlton jumped in the air and did a little jig on his way to first. As he circled the bases, Boston fans raced on to the field and Carlton had to push his way to home plate.

Even though his team lost, Sparky Anderson appreciated the quality of the game. "It was probably as good a game as I've seen. And that catch by Evans was as good a catch as you'll see." Joe Morgan saw things from a different perspective. "I was out there looking to win. We had the championship within our grasp and let it slip away. But we'll be back tomorrow night."

Pete Rose, though, probably summed up the game best for most of the players and fans at Fenway and the millions who watched it on TV when he said, "I don't think that anybody can ask for a better game than this. It had more ups and downs than any game in my life."

Boston took an early lead in the final game with three runs in the third inning. Carbo, starting in left field, drew a one-out walk and moved to third on Doyle's single. Yaz singled Carbo home and took second as Griffey tried but failed to throw Doyle out at third. Gullett walked Fisk so that the southpaw could pitch to lefty Fred Lynn and the strategy worked perfectly as Gullett struck out Lynn for the second out. But then he lost his control and gave up bases-loaded walks to Petrocelli and Evans. After the inning, Petrocelli walked out to third base, thinking, *We have it. This is our year.*

The Reds threatened in most innings but didn't score against Bill Lee until the sixth. Pete Rose started it with a single and after Morgan flied out, Bench grounded to Burleson for what should have been an inning-ending double play. But they only got the force on Rose because he slid into Doyle at second, which caused Doyle to throw wildly to first. Then Perez came up and hit a two-run homer over The Wall. They tied the game in the seventh on an RBI single and had a chance to blow Boston away, but Bench fouled out to Fisk with two outs and the bases loaded.

Rookie southpaw Jim Burton came in to pitch the eighth and walked Griffey. Geronimo sacrificed him to second and a ground-out moved him to third with two out. On a 3-2 pitch, Rose walked. Morgan came up and the count went to 1-2. Burton threw a slider low and away from the left-handed Morgan, who swung and hit the ball off the end of his bat. It was a softly hit ball that fell just out of the reach of the hard-charging Fred Lynn. Griffey scored from third as the Reds took a 4-3 lead. Both Burton and Morgan agreed that it had been a good pitch. "Two years ago, I would have struck out on it," said Joe, after the game.

In the ninth, Will McEnany quickly retired two pinch-hitters and then up to the plate came Yaz. In his 15 years with Boston, Yaz had won countless ball-games that seemed lost. He stepped into the batter's box and cocked his bat. McEnany made his pitch and Yaz swung and lifted a fly ball to center that settled in Geronimo's glove.

And just like that, the game and the World Series were over. Two splendid teams had battled each other to the final out and had provided baseball fans everywhere with a Series to warm their memories.

Pete Rose was ecstatic. "I've never won anything before. I've never won an American Legion championship. I never won a high school championship." Pete had his championship and, after a 35-year wait, so did the city of Cincinnati. It had been a long time coming!

CHAPTER 3

It's Never Over
Until It's Over

In the year 1985, some of the greatest baseball players in history reached career milestones. Pete Rose stroked hit Number 4,192, breaking the record for most hits in a career, which had been set by Ty Cobb and had gone unchallenged since 1928! Nolan Ryan became the only pitcher to record 4,000 strike-outs. Rod Carew became only the 16th player in history to get 3,000 hits; Tom Seaver became only the 17th pitcher to record 300 victories; and on the last day of the season, 46-year-old Phil Niekro became the 18th when he shut out the Toronto Blue Jays. (He also became the oldest player ever to pitch a shutout in the major leagues.)

It was also a year of achievement for younger players such as: Vince Coleman, who established a new base-stealing record for rookies by swiping 110; and Dwight Gooden, the phenomenal pitcher for the Mets, who established all sorts of records and became the youngest pitcher ever to win 20 games in a season. (He wound up 24-4).

Nineteen eighty-five was also a year of exciting divisional races (three of the four weren't decided until the next-to-last day of the season) that produced four surprise winners. Most experts thought that California or Chicago would take the American League West, while Detroit, who had pulverized the A.L. East in 1984 and gone on to win the World Series, was considered likely to repeat. In the National League, San Diego was picked to repeat in the West, while in the East, it looked as if the Cubs would battle it out with the Mets. The experts were in for a surprise.

The Kansas City Royals won the A.L. West over California by beating the Angels three out of four games in the last week of the season. Their opponents in the league championship series were the Toronto Blue Jays, who captured their first divisional title. They held off a late charge by the Yankees by beating them on the next-to-last day of the season to win the A.L. East. In the National League, the Cubs were never a factor and the St. Louis Cardinals won by holding off the Mets in another close race. The L.A.

Dodgers, winners in the National League West, were the only team to coast in, as they finished a comfortable five and one-half games in front of Cincinnati.

Kansas City was viewed as the weakest of the four play-off teams. Their offense was almost totally dependent upon George Brett, their all-star third baseman. During the season, Brett had batted .335 (second best to Wade Boggs's .368 in the A.L.), hit 30 homers, and driven in 112 runs. First baseman Steve Balboni had provided power with 36 homers, but hit only .243. Hal McRae, the DH (designated hitter), centerfielder Willie Wilson, and second baseman Frank White, who, along with Brett, formed the nucleus of the offense, had all had disappointing seasons. The team batting average was next to last in the A.L. They did, however, have a fine group of starting pitchers, led by Bret Saberhagen (20-6) and Charlie Leibrandt (17-9), as well as veteran reliever Dan Quisenberry, who led the A.L. with 37 saves.

The only problem for K.C. was that Toronto also had fine pitching as well as the second-highest team batting average in the majors. Their outfield was especially strong as George Bell (left), Lloyd Moseby (center), and Jesse Barfield (right) had combined for 73 homers and 249 RBI's.

In Game 1, Leibrandt, who had been 2-0 against the Jays during the season, started against Toronto ace Dave Stieb, who had been 0-3 against K.C. Naturally, Toronto lowered the boom on Leibrandt by scoring five runs within the first three innings, while Stieb limited the Royals to three hits in eight innings. Toronto coasted to a 6-1 win as the eighth and ninth hitters, catcher Ernie Witt and short-stop Tony Fernandez, each knocked in a pair of runs.

In game two, Willie Wilson gave K.C. an early lead with a two-run homer and catcher Jim Sundberg doubled home another run for a 3-0 lead. Toronto came back to tie the game with the help of errors by Brett and pitcher Bud Black and a two-run single by Barfield. The Jays took the lead in the eighth when Moseby came in to score after he singled, stole second, and went to third on a bad throw by Sundberg. In the top of the ninth, though, pinch hitter Pat Sheridan put one over the fence to tie the game. In the top of the tenth, Willie Wilson singled, stole second, and scored the go-ahead run on a single by Frank White. K.C. needed only three outs to even the play-offs and they had Quisenberry, who had three saves against the Jays in the regular season, in there to do the job. But Fernandez singled and came around to score on a Moseby single to tie the game. Moseby advanced on an error by Balboni when Quisenberry tried a pick-off play, and pinch hitter Al Oliver singled him home with the winning run. The extra-inning, come-from-behind win gave Toronto a 2-0 lead and put K.C. on thin ice.

But George Brett put on an amazing performance in game three to put K.C. on safer footing. He began by homering in the first and then doubled and scored in the fourth to give K.C. a 2-0 lead. Toronto stormed back, though, with five in the fifth. Barfield got them going with a two-run homer. Damaso Garcia doubled and Moseby followed with a hard smash that hit the heel of Saberhagen's left foot and then bounced into the outfield. Garcia raced home while Saberhagen lay on the ground in obvious pain. The next batter was Rance Mulliniks, who hit another two-run homer as Toronto took a 5-2 lead and Saberhagen left the game. After Sundberg hit a homer to cut the lead to 5-3, Brett hit a two-run homer to tie the game in the sixth. In the eighth, Brett did it again as he doubled and scored the winning run on a bloop hit by Balboni. After the game, K.C. manager Dick Howser said of Brett, "That's a Hall of Fame performance." That performance provided Howser with his first play-off victory after 11 straight losses.

Game four was a tense pitching duel between Stieb and Leibrandt. Going into the ninth, K.C. had a one-run lead and Leibrandt had a four-hitter. But Garcia walked and Moseby doubled him home to tie the game. Quisenberry came in to pitch and Bell greeted him with a single. Al Oliver followed with a two-run double and Toronto had pulled off a 3-1 victory—they now needed only one more win.

K.C. was back on thin ice but just as it was beginning to crack, Danny Jackson froze Toronto's bats and K.C. won the fifth game, 2-0.

In the sixth game, Hal McRae knocked in a run in the first and another in the third inning, but Toronto matched them. Brett put K.C. in front for good in the fifth, however, with a homer, and the Royals scored two more in the sixth on their way to a 5-3 victory.

The pennant chase had come down to one game now and each team had its ace pitcher ready: Saberhagen for K.C. and Stieb for Toronto. But Saberhagen had to depart after three innings due to an injury and Stieb left after five and two-thirds innings because K.C. had rocked him for six runs. Jim Sundberg did the most damage with a homer, triple, and four RBI's as K.C. went on to score a 6-2 victory. The Royals had been expected to lose and had been down three games to one, but they had just kept playing as hard as they could and it was Toronto who wound up in the deep freeze while K.C. skated away with the A.L. pennant.

The Cardinals, who led the majors with 101 victories, were ready for the play-offs. Their offense combined good hitting (they tied for the league lead) with blazing speed (a league-leading 314 stolen bases). Vince Coleman, the lead-off hitter, had 110 stolen bases; he was followed by Willie McGee, who led the league in hitting (.353), drove in 82 runs, and swiped 56 bases. Tommy Herr, batting third, hit .302 and knocked in 110 runs, and Jim Clark, the cleanup hitter, smacked 22 homers and drove in 87, even though he missed a month with an injury. Their defense, which committed the fewest errors in the N.L., was anchored at shortstop by the acrobatic Ozzie Smith. He's so spectacular that he's known as the "Wizard of

Oz" for the magical way that he plays the position. John Tudor (21-8), Joaquin Andujar (21-12), and Danny Cox (18-9) were the leading starters. And Manager Whitey Herzog had five strong relief pitchers who were referred to as "The Committee," as well as strong reserves on the bench.

The Dodgers didn't appear to be quite as strong but they had two hitters, Pedro Guerrero (.320 average with 33 homers and 87 RBI's) and Mike Marshall (.293, 28, 95), who could carry a team in a short series. Their pitching staff had the best earned-run average in the majors. It had three fine starters in Orel Hershiser (19-3), Fernando Valenzuela (17-10), and Bob Welch (14-4). The main man in the bullpen was flame-throwing Tom Niedenfuer.

In game one, the Dodgers jumped to a 4-0 lead off John Tudor, who had won 11 straight games. Valenzuela shut down the Cardinals' running game by keeping Coleman and McGee off the bases. When Valenzuela weakened in the seventh and allowed a run, Niedenfuer came in and got a double play. He shut the Cards down the rest of the way and the Dodgers won, 4-1.

In game two, Coleman and McGee each got on base in the first inning, but they were both thrown out trying to steal. As Herzog said after the game, "You rely on speed, you live dangerously; but that's what got us into the play-offs." McGee did use his speed to get the first run of the game in the third when he scored all the way from second on a wild pitch. But the Dodgers answered with three in the bottom of the inning off Andujar and went on to an 8-2 romp. They now led 2-0, but Herzog wasn't overly concerned. "We're capable of winning four in a row. We just didn't play very good ball in L.A."

In game three, Coleman used his speed to help the Cards score twice and Herr hit a home run as the Cards built an early 4-0 lead. The Cards held on to win 4-2 behind the solid pitching of Danny Cox and The Committee and the sensational fielding of third baseman Terry Pendleton. Pendleton snuffed out a Dodger rally in the ninth when, with no outs and a runner on second, he made a back-handed, sprawling stab of what looked like a sure double and turned it into an out. As Dodger manager Tommy LaSorda said later, "That one changed the game."

Before the start of game four, Vince Coleman suffered an injury to his leg in a freak accident and was out of action. But his replacement, Tito Landrum, went four-for-five as the Cards rocked the Dodgers, 12-2. They broke the game open in the second by scoring nine runs (the most runs ever scored in one inning in a play-off game), and John Tudor kept the Dodgers hitters in check. The play-offs were now tied, 2-2.

The Cards took the lead in game five when Tommy Herr doubled home two runs in the first inning. Valenzuela gave up eight walks, a play-off record, but he lasted eight innings without allowing another run. The Dodgers tied the game in the fourth on a two-run homer over the left-field fence by Bill Madlock. Niedenfuer was brought in to pitch to the Cards in the bottom of the ninth and retired the first batter. The next batter was Ozzie Smith. Oz looked overmatched against the large, hard-throwing reliever, but he smacked a fastball into the right-field stands and the Cards won, 3-2. In his eight years in the majors, the switch-hitting Oz had hit only 13 homers and had never before hit one while batting from the left side. As he said happily after the game, "Sometimes the most unlikely hero emerges."

The Dodgers now trailed 3-2 and needed a win to keep their pennant hopes alive. They struck early and enjoyed a 4-1 lead into the seventh, but a two-run single by McGee cut the lead to 4-3. Niedenfuer was brought in to replace Hershiser and protect the lead. The first batter, though, was Oz, and he lined a triple down the right-field line that sent McGee in with the tying run. Niedenfuer was beginning to think that Babe Ruth must have sneaked into Oz's uniform.

Mike Marshall got the go-ahead run for L.A. in the eighth inning with a long home run. The Cards rallied in the ninth, though, when McGee singled and Oz walked. Jim Clark came up, remembering that earlier in the play-off, "Niedenfuer had blown me away." Niedenfuer decided to try and make Clark chase a bad pitch but first, "I tried to get away with a fastball to get ahead in the count." The pitch came toward the plate. "I saw the ball real well. I saw the rotation on the seam," said Clark. Clark swung and sent the ball sailing over the fence for a three-run home run. The Cards won the game, 7-5. They had captured the National League pennant.

St. Louis had beaten back the challenge of the Mets and then gone on to defeat the Dodgers soundly. Kansas City had had to struggle to win in the weakest division and then just managed to squeak by the Blue Jays. And now they would lose the regular services of their cleanup hitter, Hal McRae, because the designated hitter wouldn't be eligible in the World Series in 1985. It looked as if K.C. had gone about as far as they could go. Danny Jackson, named to start the opening game of the World Series, summed up the situation. "We know we're the underdogs. They've got speed, they can hit, they score runs, they've got good pitching. But we'll go with our best stuff and take it from there."

Their best stuff wasn't good enough for game one. After they opened the scoring with a run off John Tudor, he shut them out the rest of the way, and RBI's by McGee, Cedeno, and Jack Clark gave St. Louis the opening game, 3-1.

In the second game, Charlie Leibrandt pitched beautifully for K.C. and had a 1-0 lead and a two-hitter going into the ninth inning. McGee, though, opened the ninth by doubling past third. But Leibrandt got Smith to ground to third and Herr to pop to right. One more out to go. Jack Clark was the next batter, and he singled in McGee to tie the game. Tito Landrum, playing for the still injured Vince Coleman, doubled on a 2-2 pitch and Clark went to third. After an intentional walk, Terry Pendleton doubled home three more runs. Quisenberry was brought in and finally got the third out, but Jeff Lahti retired K.C. in the bottom of the ninth and the Cards won, 4-2. Just like that, Leibrandt had lost his shutout and then the game.

After the game, there were a lot of questions and opinions as to whether Dan Quisenberry should have been brought in sooner. K.C.'s manager, Dick Howser, naturally didn't think so. "Charlie was in complete control. His stuff was great. I liked the way he was pitching." Whitey Herzog, the manager of the Cardinals, sympathized. "Clark didn't murder that pitch, Tito hit his double off the end of the bat, and Pendleton was jammed and just got his bat on it. We didn't hit the ball well. Leibrandt deserved to win. I guess sometimes things just happen funny."

But the Kansas City players weren't doing any laughing, especially Charlie Leibrandt, and now they were down 2-0. No team had ever lost the first two games at home and then gone on to win a World Series.

The Cards, though, were dealt a bad hand before game three even began when they learned that Vince Coleman's injury would keep him out of the rest of the Series. K.C. added to their bad deal when Lonnie Smith doubled home two runs in the fourth and Frank White followed a George Brett single with a home run in the fifth. The Cards managed to score a run in the sixth, but that was the only one that Saberhagen allowed, as K.C. coasted to their first win, 6-1.

After the game, Saberhagen told reporters, "I was really nervous in the first inning. It was a big game for us."

John Tudor made everyone on the Royals really nervous after the fourth game because he threw a five-hit shutout at them while Tito Landrum and Willie McGee homered and the Cards won, 3-0. Tudor was overpowering. As George Brett, who struck out twice, said, "It was embarrassing."

Down three games to one, K.C. really had their backs against the wall. One more loss and they could start their winter vacations. But Dan Quisenberry was able to offer a humorous point of view. "I wish that we could do it some other way, but we've done it this way all year, so what's new? If we're going to win it, this would be the way to do it."

Howser gave the ball to Danny Jackson to keep the Series alive for K.C. as he had done in game five against Toronto, and Jackson came through again. He allowed only a first-inning run while K.C. rocked the Cards for six runs, including Willie Wilson's two-run triple. It was a strange game, though, because St. Louis pitchers, led by Todd Worrell's record-tying 6 in a row, struck out 15 K.C. batters. The Cards had the strike-outs but K.C. had the win and had cut their deficit to 3-2.

In game six, Whitey Herzog started Danny Cox. He had beaten the Mets in the last week of the season when a Mets victory would have tied them with the Cards. And he beat the Dodgers in game three of the N.L. championship series after the Dodgers had taken the first two. Howser answered with Charlie Leibrandt and for seven innings, neither team could score. In the bottom of the eighth, though, Leibrandt slipped a little bit and the Cards pushed across a run with two out before Quisenberry came in to get the third out.

The Royals were now down to their last three outs. To win, they would have to overcome an amazing record—through 84 games of the regular season and 7 post-season games, St. Louis hadn't lost a single game in which they had taken a lead into the ninth inning. Pinch-hitter Jorge Orta started the inning by hitting a chopper wide of first, and with a burst of speed, just beat it out. Herzog jumped up to argue the ump's call, but, of course, he lost the argument. Then Balboni was given a second chance when Clark couldn't get to his foul pop-up, and he came through with a single. Sundberg tried to sacrifice the runners but Worrell came off the mound quickly and forced Orta at third. McRae pinch-hit and was intentionally walked to load the bases. Dane Iorg, an ex-Cardinal, was sent up to pinch-hit for Quisenberry.

"That's a situation you dream about as a kid," Iorg would say after the game. "All my life, I've dreamed about hitting with the bases loaded in the ninth inning with a chance to win the game." Iorg took the first pitch for a ball. Worrell checked the runners and then burned a fastball inside that jammed Iorg, but he fought the pitch off and hit a soft line drive into right field. Concepcion, running for Balboni, scored from third to tie the game. Iorg, already at first, turned to look at Sundberg racing toward home, and Porter, blocking the plate, waiting for Van Slyke's throw. Iorg said, "I saw Sunny sliding and scoring and that's when I felt the thrill."

Kansas City had tied the Series and Bret Saberhagen sat in the dugout thinking, "Now it's my turn. Then I almost beat Sundberg to the plate I was so happy."

In the other clubhouse, Todd Worrell, the losing pitcher, wasn't happy, but he wasn't breaking furniture or complaining about the umpiring, or Clark's not catching Balboni's foul pop. He realized that he had pitched well and gained valuable experience in a pressure situation. And, he realized, "You can't always be a winner."

Game seven was expected to be a pitching duel with Saberhagen going against John Tudor. But Tudor, who had been the Cards' best and most reliable pitcher all season, didn't have it that day. He walked Balboni in the second and Darryl Motley followed with a two-run homer. Tudor, a control pitcher, walked the bases loaded in the third and George Brett accidently singled for a run while trying to avoid being hit by a pitch. Bill Campbell came in to relieve but Balboni singled for two more runs, and then in the sixth, Kansas City erupted for six more. Saberhagen never let the Cardinals back into the game. He allowed no walks and only five harmless singles as the Royals romped, 11-0.

While the team celebrated their victory, people searched for explanations. Some pointed to the pitching staff, which had shut down the Cardinals' awesome running game, while limiting them to only 13 runs in the seven games. Many of the players, including Frank White, pointed to Dick Howser and the coaching staff. "He didn't criticize us when we weren't hitting." And Charlie Leibrant noted, "This coaching staff is all positive, all upbeat. It's the kind of team I like to play for."

The 1985 Royals were a special kind of team. Maybe, as Whitey Herzog suggested, they weren't a great team. Maybe he was right when he said that they wouldn't have been good enough even to win one of the other three divisions. But people had been telling them that they weren't good enough since spring training, told them that in the middle of the season when they were seven and one-half games behind California, and again when they trailed in the last week of the season. But they came back to win the division *and* the pennant *and* the World Series after being down 3-1 each time. They never gave up on themselves; they never quit. And because of that, Danny Jackson could scream happily, "We shocked the world!"

CHAPTER 4

Most Amazing

A funny thing almost happened to the Boston Red Sox and the New York Mets on their way to the 1986 World Series—they almost watched the California Angels play the Houston Astros!

Before the Red Sox and the Mets could meet in the World Series, the Red Sox had to beat the California Angels to win the American League pennant, and the Mets had to defeat the Houston Astros to capture the National League flag.

No problem, right? W R O N G !

In the two wildest championship series since the play-off system was first begun in 1969, California and Houston stretched Boston and New York to their limits before going down to defeat. Boston, in fact, came within one single strike of losing the play-offs, while the Mets had to eke out some very exciting wins—including the longest game in play-off history—before they were able to defeat the Astros.

Both of the series will be long remembered by everyone who cares about baseball.

The Red Sox traditionally have been a strong hitting team and 1986 was no exception. Third baseman Wade Boggs, who had won three of the last four A.L. batting titles, led both leagues with a regular-season average of .357. Following Boggs in the line-up were sluggers such as Jim Rice, who hit .304 while stroking 20 homers and knocking in 115 runs; first baseman Bill Buckner, who had 18 home runs and 102 RBI's; right fielder Dwight Evans, who poled 26 home runs and had 97 runs batted in; and Don Baylor, the designated hitter, who had 31 home runs and 94 RBI's.

In 1986, the Red Sox also had something they usually lacked—a strong pitching staff, which was led by Roger Clemens. Clemens had achieved a sparkling 24-4 record during the regular season, which included a record-setting performance in which he struck out 20 batters in a single game! He was easily the best pitcher in the A.L. And he had support from other starters such as Bruce Hurst and the exciting Dennis "Oil Can" Boyd. When the starters needed help, Calvin Schiraldi, the young, hard-throwing relief pitcher would march in from the bullpen.

California was a team made up mostly of older players such as Reggie Jackson, Bobby Grich, Doug DeCinces, and Don Sutton—whose best years in baseball were behind them. No one really expected them to put up much of a fight against the younger and stronger Red Sox.

But somebody forgot to tell that to the Angels and they came within a single pitch of taking the pennant, four games to one.

In game one, the Angels shocked the Red Sox by pounding out an 8-1 victory; and they did it in Boston and against Roger Clemens. Brian Downing, who had four RBI's in the game, and the other Angels showed no respect for Roger's regular-season record.

In game two, the Sox bounced back, 9-2, behind the solid pitching of Bruce Hurst. The game was so full of errors and mental mistakes that Don Sutton remarked, "The last time I saw a game like this, our [little league] coach wouldn't take us to Tastee-Freeze for a milkshake afterwards."

The play-off series moved to sunny California but the Angels were poor hosts as they beat Boston 5-3 and took a 2-1 lead in the play-offs. Shortstop Dick Shofield and center fielder Gary Pettis, who are not usually long-ball hitters, each stroked a home run off losing pitcher Oil Can Boyd.

Boston's manager, John McNamara, sent Roger Clemens out to the mound to try and even the Series. Roger shut the Angels out for eight innings and took a 3-0 lead into the ninth inning. He needed only three more outs, but he never got them.

Doug DeCinces led off with a home run, and after Clemens retired a batter, Dick Schofield and Bob Boone singled. Clemens was taken out of the game and Calvin Schiraldi was brought in to put out the fire. But Jim Rice lost a fly ball in the lights that allowed one run to score and put runners on second and third. The next batter was walked intentionally and then Schiraldi struck out Bobby Grich for the second out. Calvin then got two quick strikes on Brian Downing. As Brian said after the game, "He had me in real trouble. I was in a hole and he knew it." But then Calvin tried to put too much on a curve ball and the pitch hit Downing, which allowed the tying run to cross the plate.

In the 11th inning, Bobby Grich singled in the winning run off Calvin and the Angels—"the Over-the-Hill Gang"—led the play-off series, 3-1. One more victory and the Angels would win the A.L. pennant from the stunned Red Sox.

In the very next game, California led 5-2 in the top of the ninth inning and were only three outs away from winning the first pennant in their 26-year history. And they had Mike Witt, their best pitcher on the mound.

With one out, though, Don Baylor cracked a two-run homer to cut the lead to 5-4. Two pitches later, Dave Henderson, with a 2-2 count, crashed another two-run homer and Boston now led, 6-5.

California came back to tie the game in the bottom of the ninth on super base running by Gary Pettis. But losing that three-run lead in the top of the 9th seemed to have taken the fire out of the Angels, and Boston won it in the 11th when Dave Henderson hit a sacrifice fly to drive in Don Baylor with the winning run. Calvin Schiraldi, who had let the Angels tie and then win the day before, retired the Angels in order in the bottom of the inning.

After the game, Don Baylor said, "I'm still emotionally high. I've never been involved in a game like this before. We were one pitch away from a long winter."

A smiling John McNamara remarked, "That baseball game was the best baseball game, the most competitive game, I've ever seen."

The teams traveled back to Boston to finish the series but California was never really able to recover from that fifth-game loss. Boston pounded out 16 hits to take the sixth game, 10-4, and clinched the series when Roger Clemens finally earned a play-off victory in an 8-1 yawn of a game.

After 14 years of managing, John McNamara had his first pennant. Bring on the National League!

The 1986 Mets were an awesome team. They had charged into first place on April 23 and stayed there for the rest of the season. On their way to the Eastern Division title, they had won 108 games and finished 21½ games in front of the second-place team, the Philadelphia Phillies. Amazing!

The Astros were a solid team at every position with good hitting, speed, and defense, and a fine pitching staff. They had had to work a lot harder than the Mets did to clinch their divisional title but by the end of the season they were on a roll. Still, most baseball watchers didn't give them much of a chance against the high-flying Mets.

The Mets, however, were brought down to earth quickly as the Astros beat them 1-0 in the play-off opener. Astro first baseman Glenn Davis, who had led the team in homers with 31 during the regular season, supplied the power with a second-inning homer off Met ace Dwight Gooden. And Mike Scott, the top pitcher in the National League in 1986, supplied the pitching, as he not only shut out the Mets but also struck out 14 to tie a play-off record.

Mike Scott, who had led the N.L. in strike-outs (306) and ERA (2.22), and who had pitched a no-hitter on the night that the Astros clinched the divisional title, completely mastered the Mets with his split-fingered fastball. Lenny Dykstra, the Mets' center fielder, expressed the view of most of the players when he said, "I've never seen anything like it in my life. It's like a whiffle ball moving in the wind."

The Mets evened the series with a 5-1 victory as Bob Ojeda, an 18-game winner during the regular season, outpitched 39-year-old Nolan Ryan, the all-time major-league leader in strike-outs with 4,277. Keith Hernandez, the Mets' great fielding and clutch-hitting first baseman, led the attack with two hits and two runs batted in. It is interesting to note that both Mike Scott and Nolan Ryan had begun their big-league careers with the Mets. (Ryan was traded to the Angels and wound up with the Astros later on, while Scott was dealt directly to the Astros for outfielder Danny Heep.)

Game three was a thriller. The Astros took an early four-run lead off Met starter Ron Darling, with two runs in the first and two more in the second, thanks to a Bill Doran homer. The Mets fought back, though, and in the sixth inning, tied the game with the help of a three-run home run by outfielder Darryl Strawberry. Strawberry hit the homer off Astro starter Bob Knepper after going hitless (0-10) against him in the regular season. Houston regained the lead in the seventh when they scored a run off Met reliever Rick Aguilera. The Astros took that slim lead into the ninth inning and handed the ball to Dave Smith, their ace reliever. Wally Backman, the Mets' scrappy second baseman, began the inning by dragging a bunt for a single. That brought up Lenny Dykstra. (Dykstra is small and thin but his nickname is "Nails", as in the expression "as tough as nails." He doesn't quit.) Dykstra found a pitch to his liking and promptly drilled a game-winning two-run homer to give the Mets a scintillating 6-5 win. The fans at Shea stood and cheered as Dykstra scored the run that gave the Mets a two-to-one lead in games.

In game four, the Mets finally managed to score a run off Mike Scott, but it wasn't enough and they lost, 3-1. Catcher Alan Ashby and shortstop Dickie Thon each homered off Met starter and loser Sid Fernandez. The play-off was tied, 2-2.

Game five was a real nail-biter as 21-year-old Dwight Gooden matched fastballs and curveballs with 39-year-old Nolan Ryan in a tense pitching duel. Ryan was magnificent during his nine innings as he struck

Babe Ruth hitting a home run in the 1932 World Series right after he had pointed his bat to the center field stands.

Enos Slaughter sliding home safely with the winning run in the seventh game of the 1946 Series. He galloped all the way from first on a single as the Cardinals beat the Red Sox.

Don Larsen throwing the final strike in the only perfect game ever pitched in a World Series. It was the fifth game of the 1956 Series and Dale Mitchell was the last batter.

Johnny Podres winding up to retire Elston Howard, the last batter of the 1955 World Series.

UPI/BETTMANN NEWSPHOTOS

*Jerry Koosman on the mound during the fifth and
final game for the Mets in 1969. They beat
Baltimore four games to one.*

6—*Carlton Fisk blasts a home run.*

Reggie Jackson hitting the second of his three homers in the final game of the 1977 World Series. The Yanks beat the L.A. Dodgers four games to two.

9—Royals ace, Bret Saberhagen, beats the Cards in 1985.

Keith Hernandez demonstrates perfect form as he delivers a key hit in game six against Boston.

Ray Knight hitting a seventh inning homer in the seventh game to give the Mets the lead.

It's Sweet Music for the Twins as Frank Viola tames the Cards.

Kirk Gibson watches his game-winning home run in Game One of the 1988 Series. Courtesy Los Angeles Dodgers.

Dave Stewart shows his winning form in game 3 victory over the Giants in 1989 World Series.

Jose Canseco gets double-barreled Bash Brothers treatment from Rickey Henderson (24) and Carney Lansford after stroking 3-run homer against the Giants.

Jack Morris punches out the Atlanta Braves.

A happy bunch of Blue Jays.

out 12 batters while giving up only two hits, including a fifth-inning homer by Darryl Strawberry. Gooden was not quite as spectacular, but he pitched courageously for ten innings—the longest that he had ever pitched—and left the game with the score tied, 1-1.

The Mets finally broke through for the winning run in the 12th inning when their catcher, Gary Carter, who was in a terrible batting slump (1-21), lined a single to score Wally Backman. Jesse Orosco, with two perfect innings of relief work, picked up his second victory.

The Mets were now ahead in the play-offs, 3-2, and needed to win only one of the last two games. But they knew that if they didn't win game six, they would have to face Mike Scott in the final game. The Mets didn't want to face Mike Scott again.

Game six would prove to be the most exciting play-off game ever, and like the fifth game of the Red Sox-Angels series, it will be remembered and talked about for as long as people enjoy baseball.

The Mets fell behind early, as the usually dependable Bob Ojeda gave up four hits and one walk in the first inning, and Houston jumped to a 3-0 lead in their park, the Astrodome. Ojeda settled down after that rocky start, and along with relief pitcher Rick Aguilera, limited the Astros to two hits and no runs through eight innings. Their efforts, though, seemed too little, too late, as Bob Knepper had limited the Mets to two hits and took the 3-0 lead into the ninth inning.

But then the fireworks began exploding! And once again it was Lenny Dykstra who lit the fuse. Lenny led off the ninth for the Mets by lining a pinch-hit triple and scored the Mets' first run on a single by Mookie Wilson. After a ground-out, Keith Hernandez lined a double to the center-field wall, which scored Wilson. That hit narrowed the score to 3-2 and Houston manager Hal Lanier replaced Knepper with his bullpen ace, Dave Smith. Smith, who had saved 33 games during the regular season, walked Gary Carter and then Darryl Strawberry on 3-2 pitches to load the bases. Ray Knight stepped up to the plate and lined a 2-2 pitch to center field, which allowed Keith Hernandez to score the tying run.

Both teams battled tensely through 4 extra innings and then in the top of the 14th inning, the Mets pushed across the go-ahead run. Houston seemed to sag. But in the bottom of the inning, center fielder Billy Hatcher hammered a long home run over the left-field fence and the score was tied again. Neither team scored in the 15th inning, but in the 16th, the Mets erupted for three runs and took a seemingly safe lead into the bottom of the inning. But the Astros answered back with two runs and were actually in position to win the game when Jesse Orosco finally struck out Kevin Bass on a 3-2 pitch to end the longest post-season game in the history of baseball.

After a remarkable game, the Mets had finally won the pennant, and if you ever wondered if major-league ballplayers get nervous, listen to Ray Knight, "I've never been under such pressure. When I came into the dugout after we had tied them in the ninth inning, my legs were shaking." Jesse Orosco, who won 3 games, including the last one, which set a post-season record for relievers, had this to say: "I always get nervous when the bullpen telephone rings and I have to start warming up. Even when we had a 20 game lead during the season, when the phone rang, I got the jitters."

All four teams had provided baseball fans with the jitters as they battled through the most exciting play-offs of all time. Roger Angell, a famous sportswriter, summed it up for everybody when he said, "We've just lived through the greatest week in baseball history."

A lot of people thought that the World Series would seem boring compared to the play-offs but they were wrong. As exciting as the play-offs had been, they turned out to be just a warm-up for the main event.

The same "experts" who had predicted that the Red Sox would wind up fourth or fifth in their division, and then predicted they would easily demolish the Angels, were now saying that Boston didn't have a chance against the mighty Mets.

Sure, the Red Sox had solid hitting and Roger Clemens on the mound, but he wouldn't pitch every day, and they were supposed to be weak on defense and not be able to run well. And because of a new rule, the designated hitter would only be used when the games were played at Boston's Fenway Park. That meant that Don Baylor wouldn't be available, except as a pinch hitter, for the games at Shea Stadium in New York. Baylor is not only one of Boston's best sluggers; he is also a special type of man who supplied the Red Sox with the kind of leadership that turns individuals into a team.

Besides, some people snickered, the Red Sox hadn't won a World Series since 1918 and they almost always found a way to lose the big game.

The Mets, on the other hand, had compiled a regular-season record of 108-54, which matched the best record in the N.L. over the past 77 years! They had solid players at every position, strong reserves, played good defense, and could run. Their pitching staff was deep with starters, four of whom had won 16 or more games, and they had two quality relievers, the left-handed Jesse Orosco and the right-handed Roger McDowell.

So, before a pitch was even thrown, the so-called experts were predicting an easy Mets win. As Boston's manager, John McNamara, joked before the first game, "If we had read the newspapers, we mightn't have shown up."

Even some of the Mets didn't show too much respect for Boston. As Lenny Dykstra said, "I'm not going to say that we have the best team, but they don't run, they don't hit-and-run, and they don't steal bases."

But Bill Buckner, Boston's 36-year-old, sore-legged first baseman, put it all in the proper perspective when he said, "It's been an exciting season and this is a dream match-up. The two best teams in baseball."

If you could have selected a dream pitching match-up for the first game of the World Series, it would have featured Dwight Gooden matching deliveries against Roger Clemens. Gooden had been the dominant pitcher in baseball in 1985 with a 24-4 record and among his many other achievements, he had become the youngest pitcher ever to win the Cy Young Award. The award is given each year to the person who is selected as the best pitcher in his league. Roger Clemens had been just as dominating in 1986 and had also achieved a 24-4 record, which helped him to win the American League Cy Young Award after the season was finished.

But dream match-ups have to wait for pitchers' tired arms, and Dwight and Roger needed another day of rest before they could take to the mound.

So the 55,076 frenzied fans who filled Shea Stadium and the millions of fans watching on television would have to "settle" for a match-up between Boston's Bruce Hurst, who had a 13-8 record during the season, and New York's Ron Darling, who had a 18-6 record.

What the fans got to see was the best-pitched game of the entire series, which the Red Sox eked out with an unearned run in the seventh. The run scored without the Sox even getting a hit! First, Darling walked Jim Rice and then he threw a wild pitch that allowed Rice to reach second base. Then Tim Teufel, who was playing second, let a ground ball hit by Sox catcher Rich Gedman go under his glove and Rice raced home with the only run of the game.

It was a heartbreaking loss for the Mets and especially for Teufel and Darling, who allowed the heavy-hitting Sox only three hits in seven innings while recording eight strike-outs. Although bitterly disappointed, Darling showed a lot of class when he was asked about the error after the game. He just looked at the reporters and said, "Tim didn't want to make the error. He didn't do it on purpose. And that's not what beat us. There hasn't been a team yet that has been shut out and won a game." And, in answering a question about Bruce Hurst, who had pitched four-hit ball and struck out eight Mets in eight innings of work, Ron said, "He just outpitched me."

Before game two began, Billy Joel sang the National Anthem and Elie Wiesel, a famous author and the winner of the 1986 Nobel Peace Prize, threw out the ceremonial first ball.

When the game began, the fans had the match-up that they wanted—Gooden versus Clemens. But the fireworks fizzled because neither Dwight nor Roger had their good stuff. The Boston bats were explosive, however, and they blasted Gooden and three relief pitchers for 18 hits and nine runs.

Dwight's downfall began in the third inning when he walked the first batter, Spike Owens. Clemens attempted to lay down a sacrifice bunt to get Spike into scoring position. But Keith Hernandez charged in toward the plate, scooped up the bunt, and threw to second to get the lead runner. Hernandez is the best-fielding first baseman in the game with nine Golden Glove awards—the most ever by a first baseman—and he makes this play routinely. But this particular time, he threw the ball wildly and both runners were safe. Boggs was up next and he lined a double to left field and the Sox had the lead. Then Marty Barrett and Bill Buckner singled and the Mets were quickly down, 3-0.

The Mets cut the lead to 3-2 in their half of the third but Dwight served up a solo homer to Dave Henderson in the fourth and a two-run homer to Dwight Evans in the fifth. Gooden was removed after the fifth inning, having given up eight hits and six runs (five of them earned). The Mets closed the gap to 6-3 in the bottom of the fifth, which caused McNamara to remove Clemens after four and a third unglamorous innings in which he allowed three runs on five hits, walked four, and struck out only three Mets. The Mets failed to close the gap against relievers Steve Crawford and Bob Stanley, but Boston added three insurance runs and won in a rout, 9-3.

So much for dream match-ups!

The Mets had dug themselves a deep, deep hole and they were stunned. As Ron Darling said, "I never thought that we'd lose two games in our home park to anyone." But they had and now they had to travel to Boston and try to win at least two games at Fenway Park to keep the Series alive.

Although most of the Mets had never played in Fenway and were therefore unfamiliar with The Wall and its other peculiarities, Davey Johnson decided that his team would benefit from a day of rest rather than from a day of practice, so the team did not get a chance to work out before the first game in Fenway.

One Met who did have experience at Fenway was Bob Ojeda, the pitcher who was being called upon to help the Mets gain their first victory. Before he became a Met in the off-season in a deal that moved Calvin Schiraldi to Boston, Bob had spent five years pitching *for* the Red Sox. Opposing him on the mound was Oil Can Boyd, who told reporters before the game that when Ojeda played for Boston, he had told Boyd that he never felt comfortable pitching in Fenway with The Wall behind him.

But it was Boyd who felt uncomfortable after Lenny Dykstra led off the game with a home run. He felt even less comfortable when Backman and Hernandez followed with singles and Carter doubled Backman home. After Strawberry struck out, Ray Knight hit a grounder to Wade Boggs at third. Hernandez was trapped between third and home while Carter lumbered into third. Boston should have tagged at least one of them out, but the rundown was handled like a Three Stooges routine and the Mets wound up with the bases loaded. Danny Heep, batting as the designated hitter, lined a single to center that knocked in Hernandez and Carter and gave the Mets a 4-0 lead. Oil Can had sprung a leak.

Boston rallied for a run in the third inning but stranded two runners as Ojeda struck out Buckner and got Rice to ground into a force-out. That would prove to be the extent of Boston's offense, as Ojeda allowed only 5 hits in seven innings and Roger McDowell finished up with two perfect innings of relief. The Mets, however, had finally begun to hit and punched out 13 hits in a 7-1 victory. Dykstra, with 4 hits, and Gary Carter, with 2 hits and three RBI's, led the Met attack.

Bob Ojeda had faced The Wall and beaten it, and the Mets now trailed by only two games to one.

Ron Darling started the fourth game for the Mets. It was a homecoming for Ron, who had grown up near Boston and who had a lot of friends and family at the game cheering for him. The cheering must have helped because he pitched out of a bases-loaded jam in the first inning and didn't allow any runs in the seven innings that he pitched.

Darling received excellent offensive support from Gary Carter, who hit a two-run homer in the fourth off Red Sox starter Al Nipper and a solo shot in the eighth. Len Dykstra added a two-run shot in the seventh when he hit a fly ball that popped out of Evans's glove and went over the fence in right field. He also received defensive help in the sixth inning from

Mookie Wilson. With Evans on first, Rich Gedman lined a hit off The Wall. Mookie played the bounce perfectly and threw Rich out at second to put the brakes on a Sox rally.

Roger McDowell came on to pitch in the eighth, but had to be rescued after he gave up two runs. Jesse Orosco came in to get the third out and shut down the Sox in the ninth to preserve the Mets' 6-2 victory. New York had evened the Series at 2-2.

Carter, after having a miserable play-off series (4-27), had finally begun to hit with three RBI's in each of the last two games. And, about Lenny Dykstra, who had only eight homers during the regular season, Davey Johnson said, "He has such great concentration now. He's in another zone."

In game five, it was Gooden against Hurst. Gooden escaped a bases-loaded situation in the first inning, but in the second, a triple by Dave Henderson and a sacrifice fly by Spike Owen gave the Sox a 1-0 lead. In the third, after Met shortstop Rafael Santana had booted a grounder, Jim Rice walked and Evans singled, and the Sox led, 2-0. Gooden was knocked out in the fifth when Rice tripled and scored on a soft single to right by Baylor. Sid Fernandez came in and struck out Gedman but the hot-hitting Dave Henderson lashed a double and the Sox led, 4-0. Fernandez shut the Sox out the rest of the way but it was too late. Bruce Hurst made the four-run lead stand up as he surrendered just two runs to the Mets, an eighth-inning homer by Tim Teufel, and another in the ninth when, with two out, Wilson doubled and Santana singled. Then Hurst struck out Len Dykstra to end the game.

The "invincible" Mets limped back to Shea stadium knowing that they had to win the next two games. They were one loss away from having their glorious season end in bitter disappointment.

Game six was, at the least, one of the most exciting games in World Series history, one that the 55,078 fans in Shea Stadium and the millions of people who watched it on TV will always remember.

The game didn't need any extra excitement, but it got some from an unexpected source in the first inning when a man with a yellow parachute dropped out of the nighttime sky and landed in the infield. Attached to the parachute was a sign reading, "Let's Go Mets."

But it was Boston that got going in the very first inning as Dwight Evans hit a two-out double to score Wade Boggs. They added another run in the second on consecutive singles by Owens, Boggs, and Barrett. Clemens had been breezing along, but the Mets broke up his no-hitter and his shutout in the fifth when, after Strawberry had walked and stolen second, Ray Knight singled him home. Wilson singled Knight to third as Evans bobbled the ball in right field and he scored the tying run while Danny Heep was grounding into a double play.

Roger McDowell pitched for the Mets in the seventh inning and began by walking Marty Barrett. After a ground-out, Ray Knight threw wildly on Rice's grounder and the Sox had runners on first and third. Barrett scored to make it 3-2 and Rice moved to second as Evans grounded out. Next, Rich Gedman lined a single to left and Jim Rice headed home, but Mookie Wilson made a beautiful throw and Gary Carter blocked the plate, making a quick tag to nab Rice at the plate for the third out.

The Mets managed to tie the game in the eighth off reliever Calvin Schiraldi when Gary Carter hit a sacrifice fly to score Lee Mazzilli. Lee had started the inning by delivering a clutch pinch-hit single.

Neither team scored in the ninth, and the fans and players felt the tension build as the game went into extra innings. Dave Henderson, who had been the big hero in Boston's comeback win against California in game five, rose to the occasion once again in the tenth and smacked a home run off Rick Aguilera. They added another run when, with two outs, Boggs doubled and Barrett singled him home with his record-tying 13th hit of the Series.

The Mets' whole season was hanging by a very thin thread, and the thread got thinner as ex-Met Calvin Schiraldi retired the first two batters. There was one out left to the Mets' season. Gary Carter was the New York batter and he looked into the Red Sox dugout. "I saw them excited, getting ready to run off the field and celebrate. I didn't want to be the last out and have to think about it until spring training." Carter singled. Rookie Kevin Mitchell came up to pinch-hit and thought, *I'm not ready to go home*. Mitchell singled.

Ray Knight was the batter as the fans began chanting, "Let's Go, Mets." Knight stood in the batter's box and remembered his grandfather's saying, "If you have grit, all things are possible." With two strikes against him, Knight delivered a single and Carter scored as Mitchell went to third. But the Sox still led 5-4 as Bob Stanley was brought in to pitch to Mookie Wilson. Mookie walked up to the plate telling himself, "Do not strike out! Please give yourself a chance. Hit the ball." The count went to 2-2 and once more, the Mets were down to their final strike. The tension rose steadily as Mookie fouled off two pitches. Stanley pitched again; it was a wild pitch and as Ray Knight took second, Kevin Mitchell raced home with the tying run. The tension rose more as Mookie fouled off two more pitches. On the next pitch, he hit a bouncer toward Bill Buckner at first. But the ball went under Buckner's glove and Ray Knight came home with the winning run. The Mets were still alive!

The fans at Shea cheered and the Mets danced with delight. An excited Keith Hernandez shouted, "It is one of the greatest comebacks in the history of baseball!" It was, in fact, the only time in the history of the World Series that a team had been down by two runs in extra innings and had come back to win.

The Red Sox were stunned. After the game, Buckner told reporters, "I saw the ball well. It bounced and it bounced and then it didn't bounce. It just skipped. I don't remember the last time I missed a ball like that, but I'll remember that one."

A capacity crowd of 55,032 fans rocked Shea Stadium as game seven got underway. Tens of millions more watched on TV sets all across America. Baseball fever had gripped the country.

If anyone thought that Boston would roll over after their heartbreaking loss in game six, those thoughts quickly disappeared when the Sox erupted for three runs in the second inning off Ron Darling. First, Evans and Gedman hit back-to-back homers and then Boggs singled home Dave Henderson.

The Mets had to climb out of yet another hole. Sid Fernandez relieved Darling with one out in the fourth and held the Sox in check through the sixth. In the bottom of the sixth, Lee Mazzilli pinch-hit for Fernandez and delivered a single against Bruce Hurst. Mookie Wilson followed with a single and Teufel walked to load the bases. Keith Hernandez lined a long single to left center and two runs scored. Carter followed with a sacrifice fly that evened the score at 3-3. The Mets' Magic had struck again and Shea Stadium echoed with the roar of their fans.

Ray Knight led off the seventh inning with a home run off Schiraldi to give the Mets the lead for the first time in the game. Dykstra followed with a single and a steal of second. Santana singled Dykstra home and McDowell sacrificed Santana to second. Joe Sambito came in to pitch, and he gave up two walks and a sacrifice fly to Keith Hernandez, and the Mets led, 6-3.

The Sox came right back, though, and scored two runs in the eighth off McDowell as Buckner and Rice singled and Evans doubled them home with a blast to left center. Orosco replaced McDowell and closed out the inning.

The Mets bounced back with two runs of their own in their half of the eighth, one of which was a home run by Darryl Strawberry.

Orosco retired three straight in the ninth inning, and the World Series was finally over. The Red Sox and the Mets had given the baseball fans of America the kind of excitement that they could treasure forever. It had been a wonderful World Series!

CHAPTER 5

From Last to First

In the entire history of baseball no team had ever gone from last place to first place in the space of a single season. In 1991 two teams, the Minnesota Twins and the Atlanta Braves, made that great leap.

After the Twins ended the 1990 season needing a periscope to see the first-place Oakland Athletics, Minnesota's general manager, Andy MacPhail, realized that the team needed a top tier pitcher and another big bat in its lineup to be competitive. So MacPhail spent some serious off-season time signing free agents Jack Morris and switch-hitting slugger Chili Davis.

The signing of Morris, who grew up in St. Paul, Minnesota, had raised a lot of eyebrows in the Hot Stove League. Although the big right-hander had been one of the top pitchers in baseball for the better part of his 14 years with the Detroit Tigers, his record had fallen off dramatically over the previous three seasons. Morris, though, seemed to find a fountain of youth in his old hometown, and he wound up winning 18 games during the 1991 season, while becoming the anchor of a starting staff that also featured 20-game-winner Scott Erickson, and Kevin Tapani, who won 16 games. Heading up the bullpen crew was Rick Aguilera, who racked up 42 saves, the third highest total in the league.

The Twins got their first hint of better things to come when they wound up leading the Grapefruit League with a 20–11 record. "We came out of spring training with the best record in baseball, so we felt we would be competitive," recalls MacPhail. The Twins, however, didn't prove they were for real until they put together a 15-game winning streak at the beginning of June, part of a 22–2 surge that vaulted them into first place on July 11. And once they grabbed hold of the top spot, the Twins never let it go. They built up an eight game lead with six weeks to play, and they finished the season with that same comfortable margin over the second-place Chicago White Sox.

What made the Twins' turnaround even more astonishing was that they played in what was baseball's best division, a division in which even the last-place California Angels played .500 ball. The Twins were solid in every phase of the game, turning in the league's third best fielding percentage and second best earned run average, while topping the league in batting average, with a .282 mark.

Chili Davis, like Morris and Domino's pizza, also

delivered as promised, pounding out team-leading totals in home runs, 29, and RBI, 93. Kirby Puckett was, as usual, the team's leading hitter with a .319 average. The Twins also received timely hitting from right fielder Shane Mack and catcher Brian Harper, both of whom batted above .300. Yet another key contributor was rookie second baseman Chuck Knoblauch, who was steady in the field and pesky at the plate.

The Twins' opponents in the American League Championship Series were the retooled Toronto Blue Jays, setting up the first all-domed championship in baseball history. Toronto general manager Pat Gillick had set about restructuring the team right after a 1990 season in which the Jays had buckled in the stretch run and had been caught from behind by the Boston Red Sox.

Gillick, who was teasingly nicknamed "Stand-Pat," because of his reluctance to make any moves, pulled off the blockbuster trade of the off-season when he sent two All-Stars, first baseman Fred McGriff and shortstop Tony Fernandez, to the San Diego Padres in exchange for second baseman Roberto Alomar and Joe Carter, a heavy-hitting outfielder. Gillick also picked the pockets of the California Angels, by grabbing Gold Glove center fielder and leadoff hitter Devon White.

White did everything he was asked to do, as he scored 110 runs and provided the Jays with 14-carat defense in the outfield. Alomar also lived up to his All-Star billing by leading the Jays in hitting, while swiping 53 bases and becoming the best fielding second baseman in the American League. And Carter, likewise, came through in a big way, as he crushed 33 home runs, drilled 42 doubles, and drove in 108 runs.

The Jays' starting pitching rotation had to be juggled when its longtime mainstay, Dave Stieb, was sidelined by a season-ending injury in May. But a trio of starters led by 16-game winner Jimmy Key and a pair of 15-game winners, Todd Stottlemyre and David Wells, helped pick up the slack. And rookie sensation Juan Guzman gave the staff a lift by reeling off a club-record 10 straight wins in the second half of the season. The Jays also survived a September injury to their bullpen ace Tom Henke as setup man Duane Ward stepped up and became the team's stopper.

Although Toronto had taken eight of the 12 regular season games they had played against Minnesota, Twins manager Tom Kelly wasn't impressed. "Showtime starts on Tuesday," said Kelly, referring to Game 1 of the ALCS. And the Twins, playing at home in the Metrodome, ran away with that first game, stealing four bases in the first three innings while building up a 5–0 lead against surprise starter Tom Candiotti. Although Twins starter Jack Morris wasn't that much sharper, relievers Carl Willis and Rick Aguilera held the Jays to one hit over the final three and two-thirds innings to nail down the 5–4 win.

Toronto, though, turned the tables in Game 2, tagging the Twins with their first postseason loss in the Metrodome after seven straight wins. Juan Guzman, with relief help from Tom Henke and Duane Ward, held the Twins to two runs while Devon White did his thing in scoring three times to lead the Jays to a 5–2 win.

The split on the road coupled with the lack of punch in the middle of the Minnesota lineup—Puckett, Kent Hrbek, and Davis had totaled only three singles and two RBI in 20 at-bats—caused the Jays to think they were in the driver's seat as the series shifted to Toronto for the next three games. "I think we have them worried," offered Roberto Alomar.

But the Twins took control of the road to the World Series by sweeping all three games at the SkyDome, beginning with an extra-inning nail-biter in Game 3. The Jays struck first, picking up one run on a Joe Carter home run, and another on an RBI double by Candy Maldonado. But the Twins picked up one run in the fifth inning and tied the score an inning later on an RBI single by Puckett. The teams stayed deadlocked until the top of the tenth when pinch-hitting Mike Pagliarulo poled a Mike Timlin pitch over the fence. Then Rick Aguilera picked up his second save of the series by setting down the Jays in order in the bottom of the inning, and the Twins led the LCS two games to one.

The Twins turned Game 4 into a 9–3 laugher as Kirby Puckett ignited a four-run fourth inning against Stottlemyre with a solo shot into the stands. "Kirby Puckett is the best player in the game today," declared Twins first baseman Kent Hrbek. "It's a real joy to go up to bat after he gets a hit and hear the other team's catcher mumbling to himself." Left fielder Dan Gladden added to the merriment with three RBI, while Jack Morris held the Jays at bay and picked up his second win. "Morris did a fabulous job," enthused manager Tom Kelly. "He showed the boys the way."

The Twins completed their three-game sweep at the SkyDome the following day as—who else?—Kirby Puckett broke up a 5–5 tie with a two-out RBI single that sent the Twins on to an 8–5 win and the 1991 American League pennant. "Even while we were losing last year, we weren't the Bad News Bears or anything," laughed Puckett, who was named the MVP of the series. "But I'm not going to say I thought we would win the pennant and go to the World Series. No, I just knew that we wouldn't finish last again."

While the happy players whooped it up in the clubhouse, general manager Andy MacPhail grew philosophical. "Every year in baseball something happens that cannot be imagined. Never in your wildest dreams do you believe you'll see things like a team going from last place to a pennant. But it happens again and again, and that's what makes the game so special."

The Atlanta Braves knew all about finishing last. They had been the caboose of the National League's western division for three successive seasons, while finishing at least 20 games off the pace for six straight seasons.

Atlanta's rapid rise from the basement to the penthouse was fueled by the sudden maturity of their young pitching staff and the off-season signing of third baseman Terry Pendleton from the St. Louis Cardinals.

Twenty-five-year-old Tom Glavine, after four mostly unproductive years, arrived as the ace of the staff, becoming one of the league's two 20-game winners and capturing the National League's Cy Young Award. "He was great from beginning to end," declared Braves manager Bobby Cox. Steve Avery, a 22-year-old flame-throwing southpaw, ranked right behind Glavine with 18 wins. And John Smoltz, after struggling early, was spectacular during the second half of the season, compiling a league-best 12-2 record after the All-Star game.

The Braves were expecting Pendleton, a two-time Gold Glove winner, to anchor their defense and supply some timely hitting. They were also counting on him to be the leader of a team of talented young players who hadn't yet learned how to become a winner. Pendleton was being asked to do a lot, but he wound up doing even more. In addition to supplying the glue that bonded the Braves' infield defense, Pendleton, hitting better than he ever had, won the National League batting title and clouted a career-best 22 home runs. Pendleton's play and positive attitude also set the performance standards for his younger teammates. "It seems as though he always gets the job done," remarked shortstop Jeff Blauser. "He finds a way to win, and that's rubbed off on the rest of us."

The Braves showed right from the get-go that they weren't going to be cellar dwellers in 1991. "It didn't take a rocket scientist to realize that they were a much better team," said Pirates manager Jim Leyland. "I knew they were for real early in the season. You could see it. You could feel it when you played them; there was a new enthusiasm there."

The new and improved Braves were breathing the rarefied air of third place at the All-Star break, 9½ games behind the division-leading Los Angeles Dodgers. Then the Braves began to turn the screws even tighter as they racked up the best record in baseball over the second half of the season. But even as they relentlessly closed the gap on the Boys in Blue, the disbelieving Dodgers didn't see the danger until it was too late. "We aren't worried about the Braves," said Dodger outfielder Darryl Strawberry. "Why should we worry about the Braves?"

But the Braves kept coming and finally drew even with the Dodgers during the final week of the season. They were still tied going into the final weekend, which saw the Braves hosting the Houston Astros and the Dodgers traveling up the California coast to battle their longtime rivals, the San Francisco Giants. And then on Friday, the Braves showed Strawberry why he should have been worried, as they took sole posession of first place by ousting the Astros 5–2 behind Steve Avery's three-hit pitching, while the Giants downed the Dodgers 4–1.

The Braves came right back to beat the Astros on Saturday for their eighth consecutive win, as John Smoltz picked up his 14th victory and center fielder Ron Gant hit his 32nd dinger. After their win, the Braves stayed on the field watching the Giants finish their shutout of the Dodgers on the large Diamond

Vision screen. As the final out was recorded, the players and the fans in Atlanta–Fulton County Stadium exploded with the joy of knowing that they had lived what seemed to be an impossible dream.

"We believed in ourselves when no one else did," declared Ron Gant, who helped to turn the team around with his second straight 30-home run, 30-stolen base season. "This was a race people will talk about for years to come," said Braves president Stan Kasten. "It was the L.A. Glamour Boys against our Cinderella team and we won. It's just incredible."

Even the Pittsburgh Pirates, who had breezed to their second consecutive Eastern Division title, were impressed. "What they did the last two weeks might have been the greatest two weeks of baseball I've ever seen," said Jay Bell, the Pirates' shortstop. And while a lot of people thought that the Pirates' previous playoff experience gave them an edge over the young Braves, Pittsburgh center fielder Andy Van Slyke wasn't one of them. "After what they've been through, I don't think there's going to be much that rattles the Braves."

But if anyone could spook the Braves then it figured to be Van Slyke and his outfield companions, Bobby Bonilla and Barry Bonds. The three sluggers, who formed the heart of the Pirates' lineup, had combined to tattoo National League hurlers for 60 home runs and 299 RBI. In addition to their big bats, the Pirates also fielded an airtight defense that featured three Gold Glove winners, Van Slyke, Bonds, and second baseman Jose Lind. Pittsburgh's starting pitching staff was another area of strength, with 20-game winner John Smiley, 1990 Cy Young award–winner Doug Drabek, and Zane Smith, who chipped in with 16 victories. The Achilles' heel of the Pittsburgh team was its bullpen, a unit whose two top closers, Bill Landrum and Stan Belinda, had combined to produce only 33 saves.

The Pirates, though, didn't need any salvage crew in Game 1 of the National League Championship Series, as they rode Drabek's dominant pitching and Van Slyke's two RBI to a 5–1 win at Pittsburgh's Three Rivers Stadium. The Braves, though, bounced right back in Game 2 behind Avery's awesome pitching and a bad-hop hit that allowed David Justice to motor home from second and pin a heartbreaking 1–0 loss on Zane Smith. "That was the finest pitching I've seen this season," raved Pirate manager Jim Leyland. "Tonight was too much Steve Avery. We probably could have played two more hours without scoring against him."

The Series' next three games were played at Atlanta–Fulton County Stadium, where the Braves had swept six straight from the Pirates during the regular season. And the Braves, behind a three-homer barrage and the efficient pitching of John Smoltz, kept their unblemished record intact through Game 3, as they pasted the Pirates 10–3. Catcher Greg Olson was the main bopper for the Braves, delighting the tomahawk-chopping, drumbeating fans with a two-run homer, a single, a stolen base, and three runs scored.

While the Atlanta fans got a kick out of waving

their toy tomahawks, and thumping their tom-toms, many Native Americans demonstrated against those actions, believing that that type of behavior was disrespectful towards Indians. "It's dehumanizing, derogatory, and very unethical," declared Aaron Two Elk, a regional director of the American Indian Movement.

The Pirates finally broke through for a win in Atlanta, taking a 10-inning thriller, 3–2. Catcher Mike LaValliere's pinch-hit single knocked in the go-ahead run and reliever Stan Belinda pitched two hitless innings to notch the Game 4 win. Then Zane Smith got himself involved in another 1–0 nail-biter, in Game 5. But this time, Smith, with a big assist from reliever Roger Mason, came out with a "W" when light-hitting Jose Lind knocked in the winning run with a fifth-inning single against starter, and loser, Tom Glavine. "This was one of the greatest games I've ever been privileged to be part of," said Van Slyke as the teams headed back to Pittsburgh.

After dropping seven consecutive games in Atlanta, the Pirates had won two straight when it counted most, while holding the Braves scoreless over the final 18 frames. More importantly, the Pirates led the LCS 3–2, and were only one win away from snaring the National League pennant.

But the Pirates never got that elusive win as first Avery and then Smoltz pulled the plug on the Pittsburgh power supply. Avery was absolutely dominating once again, as he out-dueled Drabek, 1–0. Catcher Greg Olson knocked in the game's only run with a ninth-inning double, ending the Braves' string of 26-straight scoreless innings, a new LCS record for futility. Alejandro Pena, who pitched the ninth, picked up his third save of the series, his 14th consecutive save since the Braves had acquired him from the Mets on August 29th. "I've never seen a series that has been so exciting," said Ron Gant, who scored the ninth-inning run after setting an NLCS record with his sixth stolen base. "It's had everything—home runs, stolen bases, great defense, great pitching. This is what baseball is all about. Underneath the pressure, both teams are really having a good time out there."

The Braves had a really *great* time in Game 7 as they rode first baseman Brian Hunter's three RBI and the smothering pitching of John Smoltz to a 4–0 win and the 1991 National League pennant. The Atlanta pitching staff had held the Pirates to a record-low 12 runs while racking up three shutouts. And they had also cut the heart out of Pittsburgh's lineup by limiting Van Slyke, Bonilla, and Bonds to a .200 batting average and only three RBI. "They overmatched us," admitted Pirates manager Jim Leyland. "We've got no excuses."

As the Braves arrived in Minnesota for the first two games of the World Series, both teams were still full of the sweet joy of their last-to-first accomplishment. "I couldn't have thought of a better scenario. No one picked us to do anything, but we did. Same goes for Atlanta. I'm happy for both of us," said Jack Morris. "If this isn't the greatest year in baseball, I don't know what is," added John Smoltz. "To do what we've done, what the Twins have done, that's incredible."

But despite the charged atmosphere that always attaches itself to championship contests, the 1991 World Series got off to a rather routine start. However, the capacity crowd that rocked the flag-draped Metrodome wasn't complaining about the outcome as Jack Morris and the hometown Twins beat the Braves and surprise starter Charlie Liebrandt, 5–2. Atlanta manager Bobby Cox had bristled when, before the game, reporters questioned his choice of Liebrandt. "What's the big flap about my picking Liebrandt?" barked Cox. "Avery and Smoltz haven't had enough rest. The scale tipped towards Charlie because Glavine has been tired down the stretch, and I feel he needed an extra day off."

Cox, though, may have wanted to check the weights on his scale after Twins shortstop Greg Gagne stretched a 1–0 lead into a 4–0 cushion with a three-run homer. Ironically, Leibrandt had handcuffed Gagne in his first at-bat. "He made me look sick. He got me to chase a high fastball. He threw me a fastball again in the fifth, but this time it was right over the middle and I hit it over the fence." Kent Hrbek added a solo homer in the sixth inning to close out the Twins scoring while Rick Aguilera picked up a save after Morris yielded single runs in the sixth and eighth frames. "This wasn't one of my best games," warned Morris. "I can do better."

Glavine got the start in Game 2, but he was given

a rough greeting by Chili Davis, who drilled a two-run homer in the opening stanza. Glavine grew tougher thereafter, though, while the Braves nicked Kevin Tapani for a run in the second on a sacrifice fly by Brian Hunter and then tied the game in the sixth on a sacrifice fly by shortstop Rafael Belliard.

The Braves threatened to take the lead in the eighth, putting men at the corners with one out. But Tapani turned the tide towards the Twins by retiring Gant on a pop out behind the plate and Justice on a harmless fly to right. In the home half of the eighth, light-hitting rookie Scott Leius, who platooned at third base with Mike Pagliarulo, got the joint jumping when he poled Glavine's first pitch of the inning into the left-field seats to give the Twins a 3–2 lead. Then Aguilera pitched a scoreless inning to preserve the win and pick up his second straight World Series save. "We could have won with a clutch hit," acknowledged Atlanta manager Bobby Cox. "But we didn't get one."

Instead of being discouraged by the consecutive losses, though, the Braves were determined. "We know how to play when our backs are to the wall," said Greg Olson. "We came back to beat out the Dodgers, and we were down 3–2 to Pittsburgh. We've been in this situation and we know what to do."

The Braves knew what to do in Game 3, only it took them a while to get it done. First they spotted the Twins a gift run in the opening inning when Gant and Justice allowed Dan Gladden's fly ball to drop between them for a triple. Gladden then scored the game's first run when Chuck Knoblauch hit a sacrifice fly. The Braves, though, tied the game in the second inning, added another in the fourth on David Justice's home run, and two more in the fifth on a Lonnie Smith dinger and a bases-loaded walk. Even after Kirby Puckett ended an 0–10 World Series slide with a seventh-inning home run, the Braves looked as good as gold with a 4–2 lead and Steve Avery throwing darts. But after Terry Pendleton booted Brian Hunter's eighth-inning grounder, Bobby Cox brought in Pena to pitch to pinch-hitter Chili Davis. Pena had been a perfect 14 for 14 in save situations since coming over to the Braves, but Davis undid that streak by lacing a two-run homerun into the left-field seats to knot the game at 4–4.

The teams stayed deadlocked in a tense duel until the bottom of the 12th inning when, with David Justice on second, Mark Lemke singled to left. Dan Gladden came up throwing as Justice motored home. The throw thumped into the glove of Brian Hunter who made a desperate lunge and a sweeping tag only an instant after Justice's outstretched right hand slid across the plate with the winning run. The city of Atlanta had waited 26 years to host its first World Series game, but the Braves' victory in the longest night game in Series history made the wait seem worthwhile, and cut the Twins' lead to two games to one.

The teams got twisted up in another tingler the following day, turning Game 4 into Thriller Theater, Part II. Mike Pagliarulo keyed the Twins' attack with an

RBI single in the second inning and a solo home run in the seventh off of John Smoltz. The Braves struck back with a third-inning solo pop by Pendleton off Jack Morris, and another in the seventh by Lonnie Smith. The score was still tied in the bottom of the ninth as Game 3 hero Mark Lemke drove a one-out triple into the gap in left center. "It was a horrible pitch," lamented Twins reliever Mark Guthrie. "I was trying to throw a fastball down and away, and it went up and in."

Pinch-hitter Jerry Willard then lofted a fly ball to Shane Mack, who made the catch and rifled a throw to Harper as Lemke took off from third. "I didn't get a good jump, but I was trying not to leave too soon," said Lemke. "I knew it would be a close play when I saw Harper set up." Lemke, though, raced past Harper, his foot touching the plate as Harper was spinning to make the tag.

"Two tough nights in a row with nothing but two tough losses to show for them," remarked Kirby Puckett. "That's hard to swallow. It looks to me like it's going to go seven games."

After three consecutive one-run games, the Braves had a laugher in Game 5. Atlanta scored early and often, starting with David Justice's opposite field two-run homer in the fourth that just cleared the outstretched glove of a leaping Dan Gladden. They added another pair of runs later in the inning, notched another in the fifth, and then exploded for six more runs in the seventh as Tom Glavine coasted to a 14–3 win, giving the Braves a sweep of the three games in Atlanta and a 3–2 lead in the Series.

The teams returned to Minnesota for Game 6, but the Twins now had their backs to the Metrodome wall, only one loss away from losing the World Series. Until now their best player, Kirby Puckett, with three hits in 18 at-bats, had been the Invisible Man. But with the Championship on the line, Puckett became the Twins' Main Man and put on one of the most memorable performances in World Series history.

Puckett's opening inning triple off Steve Avery knocked in the Twins' first run, and then he trotted in with the second run as Shane Mack blooped a two-out single to left field. The Braves tried to rally in the third inning when, with a runner on first, Ron Gant scorched a line drive toward the gap in left center field. Puckett, though, was off at the crack of the bat, racing the ball to the wall. And at the last possible second, Puckett leapt high against the Plexiglas wall and made a spectacular run-saving catch. "Kirby's an impact player," said manager Tom Kelly. "He makes things happen."

And when Terry Pendleton tied the score with a two-run homer off Scott Erickson in the top of the fifth, Puckett put the Twins back on top in the bottom of the inning with a long-distance sacrifice fly. The Braves tied the score again in the seventh inning, and it stayed deadlocked at 3–3 until the bottom of the 11th inning when Puckett put the game on ice by crushing a Charlie Liebrandt change-up over the fence in left center. As Puckett circled the bases, the fans in the Metrodome stood up and began chanting "Kirby, Kirby" and they didn't stop until Puckett had made his way into the Twins' locker room. "This is a game I'll never forget," said Puckett. "It was pretty awesome."

Almost before Puckett could finish taking his bows, he was upstaged by teammate Jack Morris, who turned in one of the best and most pressure-packed performances in World Series history the following day. For seven and one-third innings he and John Smoltz were locked in a scoreless duel, turning back every threat they faced. The Twins tested Smoltz early, putting two men on base in the second inning. But Smoltz rose to the challenge and knocked off Mike Pagliarulo, who had hammered him for three hits, including a home run, in Game 4. An inning later, the Twins moved a runner to third but Smoltz choked off that threat by smoking Puckett for the third out. Then Morris, Smoltz's boyhood idol, began to strut *his* stuff, working his way out of a first and third jam in the fifth by getting Terry Pendleton to pop up and then throwing a third strike past a frozen Ron Gant. As Gant tossed his bat and helmet in frustration, Morris pumped his fist in exultation.

Morris, though, had to be at his best and his luckiest in the eighth inning. Lonnie Smith opened the inning with a single and was off at the crack of the bat as Pendleton drilled a double into the gap in left center. Smith, though, lost sight of the ball for an instant and, decoyed by Twins second baseman Chuck Knoblauch, slowed down as he neared second. And that slight hesitation forced Smith to stop at third instead of steaming home with the Series' winning run.

Given that reprieve, Morris hitched up his pants and got Gant to ground softly to first baseman Kent Hrbek, who made the tag while looking Smith back to third. Morris then issued a free pass to David Justice, which set up a force at any base and brought up the slow-footed Sid Bream. And the strategy played out as perfectly as if it had been scripted by Twins' manager Tom Kelly, as Morris fed Bream a sinking forkball, and Bream hit a grounder straight to Hrbek, who started an inning-ending 3-2-3 double play. "Fortunately, he hit it right at someone," said Morris.

"All I needed was a run," said a disappointed Smoltz. "If we had gotten one run, I know I would have stopped them." But Smoltz never got that run, and after yielding only four hits in seven innings, Smoltz was taken out of the game in the eighth after two singles put Twins on first and third with one out. "I was upset about being yanked, but sometimes you have to come out," said Smoltz.

Reliever Mike Stanton bailed the Braves out of hot water, though, when, after walking Kirby Puckett to load the bases, he got Hrbek to hit a soft liner to Mark Lemke, who stepped on second to double up Knoblauch who had foolishly broken for third.

After Morris had breezed through the ninth inning, Kelly told him, "You've been great, but you're coming out." Morris, though, wasn't ready to take a shower. "I told Tom that I still had a lot left and I wanted to keep going." Kelly shrugged his shoulders and said, "What the heck, it's just a game. Go get 'em."

Morris went out and blew the Braves away in the top of the tenth, and then in the bottom of the inning the Twins finally coaxed home the run that had proved so elusive.

Dan Gladden got things started against Alejandro Pena with a broken-bat fly ball to left center that the long-haired left fielder hustled into a double. After Knoblauch sacrificed Gladden to third, Pena intentionally walked Puckett and Hrbek, hoping to set up a force play at the plate. But pinch-hitter Gene Larkin, batting for only the fourth time in the Series, foiled the Braves' plan by lofting a fly ball single to left center that landed over the heads of a drawn-in outfield, and brought in Gladden with the run that won the 1991 World Series.

The two teams had treated baseball fans to a truly extraordinary event that included five one-run cliffhangers, four of which were decided on the last play of the game. Three of the games were extended into extra innings, including the grand finale. The superstars, like Terry Pendleton, who batted .367, Kirby Puckett, and Jack Morris—the Series' Most Valuable Player—were stage center, as expected. But many of the most memorable moments were supplied by lesser lights, such as Mark Lemke, who batted .417 while playing a major role in each of Atlanta's three wins. And there was the little-known Scott Leius, who won Game 2 with a home run, and the even lesser-known Jerry Willard, who swatted the sacrifice fly that won Game 4. And, finally, there was the rarely used Gene Larkin, getting the hit that ended what was one of the most spectacular World Series of all time.

Adding to the specialness of the 1991 World Series was the respect that the opposing players developed for each other. "The only thing that could have made it better was if they had stopped Game 7 after nine innings and cut the trophy in half," suggested Mark Lemke.

"Lemmer," replied Chili Davis, "you killed us. Man, that was fun. Let's do it again next year."

CHAPTER 6

O Canada

The 1992 playoff picture looked like a replay of 1991, except for the absence of the Minnesota Twins, who were aced out by the Oakland Athletics. The Atlanta Braves and the Pittsburgh Pirates were back to battle each other for the National League pennant, while the Toronto Blue Jays had repeated as the American League's Eastern Division champions.

The Jays had become old hands at winning their division title, something they had done three times in the previous four seasons. But the Jays had never gotten to the top of the mountain, and those persistent failures had prompted people to think of the Toronto team as a bunch of quitters and underachievers. "The questions about our team's character are legitimate," said left-hander Jimmy Key, after the Jays had been trashed by the Twins in the 1991 American League Championship Series. "And people will be asking them until we finally win a pennant or a World Series."

The questions about the Jays' character had begun in 1985, when they kicked away the pennant after leading the Kansas City Royals 3–1 in the ALCS. And the questions just grew louder as the Jays' history became littered with late-season slumps and lost pennants.

In both 1987 and 1990, the Jays had gone into the last week of the season in first place, but wound up only second best. And when they had managed to maintain their leads in 1989 and 1991, the Jays had been quickly axed by the A's and then the Twins (both by 4–1 margins).

In an attempt to counter those past failures, Toronto general manager Pat Gillick continued the restructuring of the team that he had begun the previous year, trying to find the missing pieces of the puzzle that would power the Jays to their first American League pennant.

Operating under the "if you can't beat them, buy them" principle, Gillick signed Jack Morris, the pitcher who had beaten Toronto twice in the 1991 ALCS, and outfielder–designated hitter Dave Winfield, a player with Hall of Fame credentials.

The two veteran old pros had been signed for their leadership qualities as well as their playing abilities, to provide strength of character as well as talent and numbers.

Morris responded to the dual challenge by turning in a 21–6 mark, becoming the first pitcher in Jays' history to win 20 games. And when Toronto, who had taken over first place for keeps on June 19, stumbled through the dog days of August with a losing record for the month, Morris went 5–1 and became the backbone of the Jays' pitching staff.

Winfield, meanwhile, defied all expectations by drilling 26 dingers, while hitting .290 and knocking in 108 runs to become the first 40-year-old in the history of the game to crack the century mark for RBI. "The guy may be 40, but he plays like he's 28," said Jays right fielder Joe Carter. "He has everyone's respect," added catcher Pat Borders. "When he says something, you don't question it. You just go out and do it."

Despite the presence of Morris and Winfield, the skeptics were ready for a typical Jays fade when the Milwaukee Brewers caught fire and mounted a late-season charge. But the Jays maintained their cool and their place in the standings. "This is the most relaxed and confident team I've ever seen in September," stated Jays veteran Rance Mulliniks. "Getting Jack and Dave is what made the difference," declared Pat Gillick.

Although Morris and Winfield played major roles in creating that air of confidence, they had lots of assistance from, among others, All-Stars Roberto Alomar and Joe Carter. Alomar finished among the league leaders with a .310 average, 105 runs scored, and 49 stolen bases, while knocking in 76 runs and earning a Gold Glove as the best defensive second baseman in the American League. Carter, meanwhile, was the Jays' big bopper, hammering out 34 home runs and 119 RBI.

Juan Guzman, with a 16–5 record and an excellent

2.65 earned run average, ranked second to Morris among the Jays' starters. And when Guzman's shoulder became sore and Todd Stottlemyre and Jimmy Key became shaky, Gillick engineered a late-season swap with the Mets for star hurler David Cone. When the starters faltered, Duane Ward and Tom Henke were brilliant coming in from the bullpen. Ward, considered to be the best set-up man in the game, posted a 1.33 ERA over the second half of the season, while Henke went 34 for 37 in save situations and held opposing hitters to a .197 batting average.

Toronto's pitching was, in fact, the reason that Detroit Tigers manager Sparky Anderson picked the Jays over the A's. "You know what the chances are against that rotation? You might get one of them, but what are the chances that you're going to knock off two out of three? And they can always call on Jimmy Key. That is what I would call having your cake and eating it, too."

The A's first-place finish, their fourth divisional title in five years, was as much a tribute to Tony LaRussa and his coaching staff as it was to the players.

Forced to steadily shuffle his starting lineup due to a seemingly unending string of injuries, LaRussa somehow always seemed to pick the right replacement and push the buttons perfectly. The rash of injuries was so sustained that the projected starting outfield of Rickey Henderson, Dave Henderson, and Jose Canseco never got to play a single game together. By the end of the season only Rickey was on the A's active roster, while Dave was on the disabled list and Canseco was in

Texas, having been traded to the Rangers for right fielder Ruben Sierra and pitchers Bobby Witt and Jeff Russell.

The injury jinx also claimed, among many others, shortstop Walt Weiss, catcher Terry Steinbach, and first baseman Mark McGwire. McGwire, though, managed to hack 42 homers and drive in 104 runs, despite missing 23 games. In fact, only one A's player, Mike Bordick, who filled in at shortstop for Weiss and then shifted over to second, was able to play in as many as 150 games.

In addition to injuries, the age factor had also started to take its toll on the A's, and especially on its once-dominating pitching staff. "Those guys are older now," observed Toronto's Tom Henke. "I don't think they're throwing the same as they once did." And Dave Stewart, the longtime anchor of the A's staff, didn't offer any disagreement. "I just used to be able to throw smoke and a forkball to get people out. But now I have to set up the hitters," said Stewart, a former 20-game winner who had struggled to win 12 games in 1992.

The one constant and shining star on the A's pitching squad was Dennis Eckersley, who had saved 36 straight games on his way to compiling a major-league high 51 saves and earning both the Cy Young and Most Valuable Player awards. "He's the best pitcher in baseball," remarked Giants reliever Dave Righetti. "A Hall of Famer, no question."

The A's game plan against the Jays was simple:

Just get to the eighth or ninth inning with a lead and then bring in Eckersley.

Blue Jays manager Cito Gaston named Jack Morris, the star of the 1991 postseason, to start Game One at Toronto's SkyDome. Tony LaRussa countered with Dave Stewart, who carried a reputation as a big-game pitcher and a 5-0 record in ALCS play. "When you look at Stew, you're looking at a guy who's always risen to the occasion," acknowledged Gaston.

The A's mauled Morris early, with Mark McGwire crushing a two-run second-inning homer far over the left-center field fence, and the next batter, Terry Steinbach, following with a dinger down the left-field line that stretched the A's lead to 3–0. Morris managed to stymie the A's over the next six innings, which allowed the Jays to jump back into the game. Catcher Pat Borders struck the first blow with a solo homer in the fifth inning. Then Dave Winfield sliced the A's lead to 3–2 when he took Stewart downtown in the sixth inning, and became the oldest player ever to hit a home run in postseason play. Two innings later Winfield chased Stewart with a two-out double, and then came in to score the tying run when John Olerud delivered a clutch single off reliever Jeff Russell.

However, the Jays' comeback was undone by Harold Baines, who blasted a home run off Morris in the top of the ninth. And then Eckersley took to the mound in the bottom of the inning and closed out the 4–3 win, exactly as planned.

The Jays, though, evened the series the following

day with a 3–1 win behind a premium pitching performance by David Cone, and some offensive fireworks
from third baseman Kelly Gruber. Gruber, who had
suffered through a season-long slump, broke the ice
with a two-run homer in the fifth inning, and then
came around to score the Jays' final run after drilling a
double to start the seventh.

Cone, meanwhile, breezed through the first eight
innings, and when Ruben Sierra socked a ninth-inning
home run, Tom Henke came in to pick up the save.
"Winning this game gives us a huge lift," said Cone.
"We would have been in dire straits if we had lost both
of these home games."

After two tight, well-played games in Toronto, the
series moved to Oakland, where the A's proceeded to
turn in a slapstick performance that included a trio of
errors, three wild pitches, and a dreadful decision by
third-base coach Rene Lachemann, which took the
team out of a potential game-breaking rally in the second inning. "That's not the way we usually play," noted
Terry Steinbach, after the A's had thrown away the
game, 7–5.

Toronto, though, turned the screws tighter still the
following day when they mounted a late-game comeback that ripped Game 4 right out of the hands of the
startled A's. The Athletics had seemed all set to put the
game in the win column after they sent Jack Morris to
an early shower and took a seemingly safe lead into the
eighth inning. And even after the Jays had rallied and
narrowed the score to 6–4, Eckersley appeared to re-

store order with an inning-ending strikeout. "That was a big out. I thought we were all right," recalled Eckersley afterwards.

But Eckersley was all wrong because Roberto Alomar whacked a two-run homer in the ninth to tie the game, and then Pat Borders won it with an 11th-inning sacrifice fly.

The dramatic comeback gave the Jays a 3–1 edge and allowed them to feel that they were made of stronger stuff than previous Toronto teams. "I think this should dispel any ideas about this team crumbling. This team doesn't have any quit in it," said Winfield.

Dave Stewart stuck his finger in the dike with a 6–2 complete game victory in Game 5. "Stew saved them," said Winfield. "He went into his bag of tricks and pulled out something good." But then the teams returned to Toronto and the Jays opened the floodgates with a 9–2 win that earned Toronto its first American League pennant.

Joe Carter started the rampage with a two-run first-inning homer off Mike Moore. "Before the game, I told the guys to hop on my back," revealed Carter, who had been mired in a 4-for-21 slump. "I'd been riding their backs long enough." Two innings later Candy Maldonado cracked a three-run homer that sent the high-flying Jays soaring to a 6–0 lead. That was all the cushion that was needed as Juan Guzman and relievers Duane Ward and Tom Henke kept the A's in check. As soon as Maldonado caught Sierra's fly ball for the last out of the game, the Jays began an instant on-field celebration, while the loudspeakers blared a song entitled "Finally."

"We did it," said Alomar, who had at least one hit in each of the six games and was named the series' MVP. "We can celebrate tonight. But this is not finished. Now we have to win the World Series."

The Braves had had a roller-coaster season, rising and falling on the arms of their starting pitchers. When their starters faltered at the beginning of the season, the Braves dropped into the basement of the National League's Western Division. But between May 29 and August 19 Tom Glavine, John Smoltz, and Steve Avery racked up a 31–7 record, including 13 straight by Glavine, and the Braves surged into first place. Although the Big Three nosedived again towards the end of the season, rookie Pete Smith took up the slack by winning seven straight games.

"The starters have been our key all season long," declared Braves manager Bobby Cox. And they would need to be at their best in the postseason, since injuries had claimed their two top relievers, Alejandro Pena and Kent Mercker. The Braves had filled the holes in their bullpen by recalling Mark Wohlers from the minors and engineering a late-season trade for veteran Jeff Reardon, hoping that he had enough juice left in his arm to squeeze out a few more saves.

The Braves' postseason picture was further clouded when Greg Olson was sidelined by a season-ending injury in September. "Greg's loss takes something special away from Atlanta," said Los Angeles

Dodgers center fielder, Brett Butler. "He's more than just a good catcher; he's the quarterback and the heart of their team."

On the plus side for the Braves was All-Star third baseman Terry Pendleton, a Gold Glove in the field and one of baseball's best hitters. The Braves also got a big boost from two-sport star Deion Sanders, who hit over .300 and stole 26 bases as a part-time outfielder. Center fielder Otis Nixon was another sparkplug at the plate and on the basepaths, while Sid Bream and Brian Hunter were a power platoon at first base, combining for 24 home runs and 102 RBI.

When all was said and done, however, it was clear that the Braves' hopes hinged on the golden arms of Glavine, Smith, and Avery. As Bobby Cox advised, "We'll go as far as our starting pitchers can take us."

The Pittsburgh Pirates, on the other hand, rode to the top of the National League East on the backs of a pair of heavy-duty hitters, center fielder Andy Van Slyke and left fielder Barry Bonds.

Van Slyke finished as the runner-up to San Diego Padres third baseman Gary Sheffield in the race for the National League batting title, and was among the league's leaders in 10 offensive categories. Bonds, meanwhile, was in a league of his own, finishing at the top of the lists in runs, walks, extra-base hits, on-base percentage, and slugging percentage, while placing in the top 10 in five other offensive categories. "Barry is this year's MVP," declared Houston Astro scout Charlie Fox. "No discussion. No argument. End of debate."

Atlanta manager Bobby Cox took his praise of Bonds a step further. "Barry is the best player in all of baseball."

Van Slyke and Bonds were also great outfielders, and along with second baseman Jose Lind gave the Pirates three Gold Glove defenders. As Chicago Cubs manager Jim Lefebvre noted, "The Pirates don't beat themselves."

But as superior as the hitting and fielding were, that's how suspect the pitching was. Somehow, manager Jim Leyland had stitched together a staff whose leader, Doug Drabek, won only 15 games and that counted on rookie Tim Wakefield, a midseason call up, to make a major contribution.

Leyland had played a major role in leading the Pirates to their third consecutive divisional title. He had kept the team focused on winning throughout the long season, while he juggled a lineup that had lost both 20-game winner John Smiley and 100-RBI-man Bobby Bonilla to free agency.

Leyland knew that the key to the Pirates' chances in the LCS was for Bonds and Van Slyke to step up big-time against the talented trio of starters that the Braves would throw at them. "It all boils down to this: We'll go as far as our hitters can take us."

The only problem with depending upon the Doomsday Duo was that they had played like duds in the past two Championship Series, especially Bonds, who had hit for a .156 average while driving in only one run in 13 previous playoff games.

John Smoltz, to the delight of a capacity crowd at Atlanta–Fulton County Stadium, stifled the Pirates' offense and sent Bonds' playoff average even further south as he easily bested Doug Drabek in Game 1 of the National League Championship Series. Picking up where he had left off in the 1991 postseason, Smoltz pitched Atlanta to a 5–1 win while receiving Play-of-the-Day defensive support from second baseman Mark Lemke and Terry Pendleton, who backhanded a tracer down the third-base line and turned it into a 5-4-3 double play. "They make plays like that behind the kind of pitching they got, and they become terribly tough to beat. In fact, they'll bury you," said Leyland.

Which is exactly what the Braves did to the Pirates in Game 2. Atlanta began the avalanche with a four-run second inning against southpaw Danny Jackson, and they continued piling it on in the fifth, when left fielder Ron Gant hit the first grand slam of his big-league career. And when the Pirates awoke from their stupor by pushing across four runs in the top of the seventh inning, the Braves answered right back with five of their own in the bottom of the frame. "It had been the one time we had felt good about ourselves, and then it was taken away so quickly," lamented Van Slyke. "It was embarrassing," said Leyland, summing up the 13–5 loss.

As the series shifted to Pittsburgh's Three Rivers Stadium, the Pirates were down 2 games to 0 and needing a win to stay in contention. The Pirates, though, seemed overmatched as they sent out rookie Tim

Wakefield to duel against 20-game winner Tom Glavine. But Wakefield baffled the Braves with his knuckleball, while Van Slyke joined the living with a seventh-inning sacrifice fly that gave the Pirates a 3–2 win. Atlanta shortstop Jeff Blauser summed up the frustration that he and his teammates felt in trying to hit the wiggly-squiggly knuckleball: "You'd think they'd allow us to use tennis rackets; we'd have a lot better chance that way."

It was Smoltz against Drabek, again, in Game 4, and although neither pitcher had his best stuff, Smoltz did put his bat to good use. "The only way I got to stay in the game was because I singled home a run to keep things close," joked Smoltz, who still trailed 3–2 at the end of three innings. Smoltz singled again in the sixth, sparking a two-run rally that gave the Braves a 6–4 victory, and tied him with Hall-of-Famer Steve Carlton as the winningest pitcher in NLCS history, with four.

The Braves, with a 3–1 lead in games, had forced the Pirates' backs to the wall. And they also had what looked to be a mismatch on the mound for Game 5, with Steve Avery starting against self-described utility pitcher Bob Walk. But expectations got turned upside down as the Bucs bombed Avery for four first-inning runs, while Walk pitched the game of his life, holding the Braves to only three hits in a complete game 7–1 win. Barry Bonds contributed to the first-inning festivities with an RBI double, his first postseason run batted in since 1990. "I couldn't understand what was going on," said Bonds afterwards. "I didn't know how I could be outstanding for 162 games and then disappear for seven—three years in a row."

The series switched back to Atlanta, but the Bucs didn't miss a beat, as they once again avoided elimination by battering the Braves, 13–4, behind Tim Wakefield. The Pirates ended the suspense early, with an eight-run second-inning outburst against Tom Glavine. Bonds began the barrage with a home run to right center and shortstop Jay Bell put the icing on the cake with a three-run homer over the left-field fence. Before the inning was over, Bonds had hacked his second hit and Glavine was taking a shower. "I stunk. That's it. It all happened so fast that I don't even know what happened."

The Braves had let the Bucs off the ropes, turning the LCS into a one-game, winner-take-all season, with John Smoltz facing off against Doug Drabek. Smoltz pitched six strong innings, yielding one run in the first inning and another in the sixth on a Van Slyke single. Drabek, though, was even tougher as he shut out Atlanta on only five hits through eight innings.

It was last call for the Braves as Pendleton opened the bottom of the ninth with a fly ball double that landed just inside the right-field foul line. That brought up David Justice, who had made the defensive Play-of-the-Day an inning earlier when he gunned down Orlando Merced, who had tried to score from first on a Jeff King double. Justice hit a routine grounder at Jose Lind, the league's top defensive second baseman. "He makes that play 10 times out of 10," said Leyland. But this particular time Lind bobbled the ball and Atlanta now had runners at the corners. Drabek then walked Bream to load the bases and Leyland decided he had to bring in Stan Belinda. "You could tell that Doug didn't have anything left at that point," said Leyland. Belinda's first pitch became a sacrifice fly by Ron Gant that cut the Bucs lead to 2–1. After another walk filled the bases, Belinda got Brian Hunter to hit an infield pop fly to Lind. "After we got that second out, I felt like the game was ours," revealed Leyland.

With the pennant on the line, Cox sent up Francisco Cabrera, a little-used reserve catcher, to pinch-hit. Cabrera, who had been to bat just one other time in the series, and only 10 times during the entire season, bounced a 2–1 pitch into the hole between short and third. As Justice trotted home with the tying run, the slow-footed Bream was lumbering around third. "I went as hard as I could." At the same instant that Bream turned for home, Barry Bonds fielded the ball and uncorked a strike to catcher Mike LaValliere. But Bonds' throw was a heartbeat too late to nab the sliding Bream, and the Braves snatched the pennant from the Pirates in a swirl of white chalk and dust. "I was just trying to make contact," said Cabrera afterwards. "The next thing I know I was standing at first base yelling, 'He's safe! He's safe!' I don't remember anything else, just that we won and I'm the big hero!" added Cabrera with a big smile on his face. The win allowed the Braves to become the first back-to-back pennant winners since the Los Angeles Dodgers turned the trick in 1977–78.

In the other clubhouse, Leyland sat stunned at the sudden reversal of fortunes, which had united the Pirates with the Philadelphia Phillies and Kansas City Royals of 1976–78 as the only teams to lose three consecutive LCS's. "I'm still in shock. This is without a question the toughest loss I've ever had to handle." After he had had a few minutes to cool down, Leyland continued, "It's tough, but it's life. And you have to learn how to handle winning and losing."

John Smoltz, who was named the NLCS Most Valuable Player, joined with his teammates in paying respect to the Pirates. "Drabek pitched his heart out, and you have to credit the Pirates for everything they did. It was just a situation where we never stopped fighting. It was a miracle win, but we'll take it and go to the World Series."

There were a lot of "firsts" surrounding the 1992 World Series. The Blue Jays had finally won their first pennant, which made their manager, Cito Gaston, the first black man to lead a team to a league championship. Toronto's win also meant that, for the first time ever, a team from outside the United States would be playing in a World Series.

For the Braves, though, Game 1 looked like a scene out of *Nightmare on Elm Street*. Instead of Freddy Kruger, though, the Braves were facing Jack Morris, the pitcher who had killed them off with a 10-

inning shutout in the seventh game of the 1991 World Series.

Morris, who carried a 4–0 record and a 1.54 ERA in World Series play into the game, was wearing a new uniform, but he was up to his old tricks, as he mesmerized the Braves for the first five innings, and ran his consecutive scoreless inning streak to 18, one shy of the record set by Bob Gibson of the St. Louis Cardinals in 1967. But the string was broken in the sixth, when Braves catcher Damon Berryhill, playing in place of the injured Greg Olson, crashed a three-run homer off Morris. "It was a forkball," explained Morris. "A 390-foot forkball that didn't do anything."

That was all the runs the Braves would get, but it was more than enough, because Tom Glavine was in a groove, limiting the Jays to four hits and one run, a fourth-inning home run by Joe Carter. The win delighted the hometown fans and was a big boost for Glavine, who had carried the baggage of a 1–5 record and a 12.27 ERA in postseason play into the game. "Sure there were people wondering why I was out there starting," said Glavine, who was coming off his eight-run disaster against the Pirates. "But I never lost confidence in myself and I know my teammates didn't either."

Game 2 got off to an ominous start for Toronto even before it had officially begun, when a United States Marine color guard accidentally flew the Canadian flag upside down while the U.S. and Canadian national anthems were being performed. The mistake provoked a big response from Canadians who witnessed the incident on television, some of them reacting with annoyance, while others found it amusing.

And once the game did begin, John Smoltz got off to a super start, striking out five of the first six Toronto batters, while the Braves were building a 2–0 lead. The Jays scratched out two runs off Smoltz in the top of the fifth, but the Braves immediately untied the game in the bottom of the inning with a two-run rally of their own. Deion Sanders, who was starting in left field in place of Gant, ignited the scoring with a single to right. The fleet-footed star then stole second and continued on to third on catcher Pat Borders' throwing error. After Pendleton drew a walk, Justice came through with an RBI single to score Sanders and finish off Cone. The Braves then stretched their lead to 4–2 as pinch-hitter Brian Hunter hit a sacrifice fly off of David Wells. While a succession of four Toronto relievers kept the game in reach by holding Atlanta scoreless for the remainder of the game, the Jays sliced the Braves' lead to 4–3 on an eighth-inning RBI single by Winfield. But Jeff Reardon prevented any further damage by striking out Kelly Gruber to end the inning. It was Gruber's 22nd straight out in postseason play, tying a record set by Cardinals shortstop Dal Maxvill in 1968 and equaled by Dave Winfield in 1981 when he played for the New York Yankees.

Reardon retired the first batter in the ninth inning, but then he made a major mistake and walked pinch-hitter Derek Bell. "You can't walk a guy in that situation," acknowledged Reardon afterwards. And then The Terminator made the fatal mistake of taking pinch-hitter Ed Sprague too lightly. The Braves scouting report had warned that Sprague was a low fastball hitter, but Reardon hadn't paid too much attention to it. "He's not somebody who usually gets to hit in that situation, so I wasn't that aware of him," admitted Reardon.

· Sprague made Reardon pay for his lack of attention by tattooing The Terminator's first pitch, a low fastball, over the fence to give the Jays a 5–4 lead. "I dreamed about doing that as a kid," said Sprague, who had only one home run during the season. "Every kid dreams it. But having it come true, that's a different story."

Then Tom Henke came in and set the stunned Braves down in the bottom of the ninth, saving the first-ever World Series win for Duane Ward and the Toronto Blue Jays.

The Jays were juiced by Sprague's big blast, and hoped that it would set the tone for the rest of the Series. "We know what a home run like this did in Oakland when Robbie connected off Eckersley," said Winfield. "That gave us a great lift. Now we just have to go home and get it going up there."

The fans in the SkyDome were all set to welcome the first World Series game ever to be played outside U.S. borders. And the fans were also ready to remind the Marines about their blunder in the previous game, with many of them showing up wearing T-shirts and waving pennants that pictured the U.S. flag upside down. But an international incident was adroitly averted when a different Marine color guard managed to fly the Maple Leaf rightside up while the Royal Canadian Mounted Police correctly hoisted the Stars and Stripes. The capacity crowd roared its approval and the umpire screamed, "Play ball!"

Over the first three innings of play, starters Juan Guzman and Steve Avery kept the hitters shackled. But in the top of the fourth, Sanders and Pendleton touched Guzman for back-to-back singles to start the inning. Then David Justice jumped all over a Guzman pitch and sent it winging to straight-away center. Devon White, the three-time Gold Glove center fielder, was off at the crack of the bat. White raced back as far as he could, leapt, and made a spectacular over-the-shoulder catch an instant before he crashed into the Plexiglas fence. "There are good, great, and awesome catches. That's a new category—above awesome," declared Andy Van Slyke, who watched the game on television.

The catch became an instant double play as Pendleton, running all the way, was called out for passing Sanders; and the Jays just missed turning it into the second triple play in World Series history. After the catch, White whipped the ball to first baseman John Olerud, not realizing that Pendleton had already been called out. At that point, Sanders decided to tag up and try for third, but he had to beat a hasty retreat when Olerud alertly pegged the ball to Gruber. Gruber ran Sanders back towards second, the way he was taught in

Little League. But instead of throwing the ball to short-stop Manny Lee, Gruber tried to catch the speedy Sanders, who slid safely back into second.

Joe Carter got the Canadian crowd clapping again in the bottom of the fourth when he crushed an Avery fastball over the left-field fence, giving the Jays a 1–0 lead and a record for having hit home runs in nine consecutive postseason games.

The Braves, though, tied the score in the sixth on a double by Sanders and an RBI single by Justice, and went ahead in the eighth, 2–1, when an error by Gruber allowed Atlanta to score an unearned run. But as quickly as Gruber gave the gift away, he snatched it back, smacking a leadoff homer in the bottom of the inning to knot the score at 2–2.

After Duane Ward disposed of the Braves in the top of the ninth, Roberto Alomar opened the bottom of the inning by hitting a single off Avery, and promptly stealing second. Cox brought in Mark Wohlers, who walked Carter and gave up a sacrifice bunt to Winfield. With runners now at second and third, Cox went to his bullpen again, bringing in Mike Stanton, who intentionally walked pinch-hitter and Game 2 hero Ed Sprague to load the bases. The wheels kept turning as Cox called in Reardon to terminate the Jays' uprising. Reardon got two quick strikes on Candy Maldonado, but then the Candy Man put his bat on the ball and lifted a fly ball past the drawn-in outfield while Alomar trotted home with the run that gave Toronto a 3–2 win and a 2-games-to-1 lead in the Series.

The Braves had lost two successive one-run games, and life wasn't about to get any easier as they were forced to face a pumped-up Jimmy Key. "This is the biggest start of my career," declared Key, who had become the forgotten man on the staff since David Cone had come to town. "This game means everything to me," said Key, right before he locked up in a duel with Tom Glavine.

Glavine was sharp, giving up only six hits and two runs, the first on a third-inning home run by Pat Borders that stayed just inside the left-field foul pole, and the second on an RBI single by Devon White in the seventh.

Key, though, was a shade sharper, surrendering only five hits and a single run in seven and two-thirds innings. When Key was removed in the eighth, Duane Ward and Tom Henke made the razor-thin margin stand up by securing the final four outs, and giving the Jays a 3-games-to-1 lead.

The Game 5 matchup reunited Jack Morris and John Smoltz, the starting pitchers in the classic seventh game capper to the 1991 World Series. What a difference a year can make! Just 12 months earlier, Morris had earned the World Series MVP Award for pitching the Minnesota Twins to the title, running his 1991 postseason record to 4–0. This time around, though, Morris had an 0–2 record in championship play and was sporting a really ugly 7.43 ERA. Morris, however, wasn't about to bow his head in shame. "I'm not pleased about my record in the postseason this year, but I've done the best I could. If I was a robot, I'd throw perfect games every time out and at the end of the season I'd retire because I'd be bored to death."

Morris didn't have to worry about boredom or perfection in Game 5, however, as the Braves broke out of their series-long slump and battered yesterday's hero for seven runs in four and two-thirds innings.

Designated hitter Lonnie Smith drove Morris from the mound by drilling a fifth-inning grand slam over the right-field fence, but the Toronto fans delivered the final blow when they started booing Morris. "People forget real quick," snapped an angry Cito Gaston afterwards. "Jack won 21 games for us this year." Morris, though, just shrugged off the fans' behavior. "If booing bothered me, I would have left the game a long time ago. I think my sister booed me once when I made an out in Little League."

The overdue show of power by the Braves was welcome news for Smoltz, who had no wins to show for his three previous World Series starts over the past two years, despite a glittering 1.66 ERA. "I guess John was wondering when we were going to score him some runs," smiled Otis Nixon, who had contributed three hits and two runs to the Braves' 7–2 win.

The Jays had let the Braves slip off the hook in Toronto, and now they had to try to reel in the World Series in Atlanta.

Game 6, following the pattern created in the first four games, turned into a tension-packed game as the Jays took a 2–1 lead into the bottom of the ninth inning.

Tom Henke, the Jays' fifth pitcher of the day, was on the mound trying to tie down the championship for Toronto, while the Braves' Otis Nixon, with two on and two out, was trying to tie up the series for Atlanta. "I wanted that shot," revealed Nixon. "I wanted to be the guy." Nixon met the challenge by slapping a single into left field that scored Jeff Blauser and knotted the score at 2–2.

The teams then battled into the top of the tenth inning, when with one out, Charlie Leibrandt, the fifth Braves hurler of the game, hit Devon White with a pitch and gave up a single to Roberto Alomar. With two right-handed batters due up, Atlanta manager Bobby Cox could have called on Jeff Reardon, who was all warmed up in the Braves' bull pen. But with Reardon's failures in Games 2 and 3 fresh in his mind, Cox elected to let the left-hander stay in the game.

Leibrandt coaxed the second out of the inning from Joe Carter, getting the Jays slugger on a harmless fly to center. That brought up Dave Winfield, hitting in the type of spot for which Toronto had signed him. It was also a chance for Winfield to finally recover from his 1-for-22 fadeaway in the 1981 World Series, the one stain on his long and brilliant resume that included 432 home runs and 1,710 RBI. It was also an opportunity for Leibrandt to ease the painful memory of the game-losing gopher ball he had served up to Kirby Puckett in Game 6 of the 1991 World Series. The count went to 3–2, and then Winfield drilled a double down the left-field line, driving in White and Alomar with the runs that gave the Jays a 4–2 lead. As Winfield stood on second base, pumping his fist into the air, he was thinking, "This was my biggest game, my best day in baseball."

But the Braves still had one more turn at bat, and they did not intend to go gently into the night. They quickly nicked Jimmy Key for one run, and with two outs advanced pinch-runner John Smoltz to third base, 90 feet away from retying the game. Gaston brought in Mike Timlin to pitch to Otis Nixon, whose clutch hit had sent the game into extra innings. Joe Carter trotted over to Timlin to remind him that Nixon ran like a greyhound and was a threat to drop a bunt. "This guy will lay it down. You've got to *bounce* off the mound."

Timlin, in only his second season in the big leagues, tried to calm himself by pretending he was back in the minors. "Just relax and throw strikes," he told himself. On Timlin's second pitch, Nixon flicked his bat at the ball, trying to push a bunt past the pitcher. But Timlin bounced off the mound, fielded the ball and threw it to first baseman Joe Carter for the out that gave the Toronto Blue Jays its first World Series.

And for the first time in baseball history, a team from outside the U.S. had won the World Series. "This organization wanted a championship," declared David Cone. "And it went after it with all it had. They put all the pieces in place."

CHAPTER 7

Return Ticket

In the 1993 season, form held fast in three of the four divisional races. In the American League East, the defending world champion Toronto Blue Jays teased the New York Yankees and Baltimore Orioles into September. But then the Jays closed the regular season by winning 17 of their final 21 games to finish seven games in front of the second-place Yankees and capture their third consecutive divisional title.

In the AL West, the Chicago White Sox also stumbled in early September before they lived up to preseason expectations to finish eight games in front of the Texas Rangers and win their first divisional title in ten years.

Meanwhile, in the National League West, the Atlanta Braves came out on top as expected, but it wasn't the cakewalk that most people thought it would be, despite the fact that Atlanta topped the major leagues by winning 104 games. [Author's note: I have used the name "Braves" once, for identification purposes. But because many Native Americans object to the use of team names such as "Braves" and "Redskins," I have chosen to repect their wishes and not use the name again.]

The only surprise divisional winner was the Philadelphia Phillies, who had finished at the bottom of the NL East in 1992 and who hadn't won a divisional title since 1983. But the Phils shot out of the starting blocks like Carl Lewis, winning 45 of their first 62 games. Then they withstood a late charge by Montreal and finished three games ahead of the Expos.

The 1993 version of the Blue Jays was a vastly different team than the one that had brought Toronto its first World Series only a year earlier. The Jays had lost a host of players to free agency, including designated hitter Dave Winfield, who had delivered the Series-winning hit in 1992. Gone, too, were starting pitchers David Cone and Jimmy Key, as well as Toronto's top closer, Tom Henke. Also among the missing was Jack Morris, a twenty-game winner in 1992 who had been ineffective early in the year and had then suffered a season-ending injury.

But Blue Jays' general manager, Pat Gillick, Toronto's master builder, hadn't been idle. He had shored up the starting pitching staff by signing veteran Dave Stewart, and even after the season was well underway Gillick kept dealing. First he picked up shortstop Tony Fernandez, a former Jay, in a swap with the New York Mets, and then he added left fielder Rickey Henderson in a trade with the Oakland A's. Although Henderson disappointed by hitting only .215 for the Jays, Fernandez provided a big lift by hitting .306 and driving in 50 runs.

But Gillick's prize pick-up was Paul Molitor, who had had an outstanding fifteen-year career with the Milwaukee Brewers. Molitor responded to his new surroundings by posting personal bests in home runs (22) and RBI (111) while finishing second in the AL in hitting with a .332 batting average.

Finishing ahead of Molitor for the AL batting title with a .363 average was Jays first baseman John Olerud. And when second baseman Robbie Alomar finished third at .326 the Jays became only the second team in baseball history to sweep the top three spots in a league batting race.

The big thumper for the Jays was right fielder Joe Carter, who had swatted 33 dingers and driven in a career-best 121 runs. "He's a quiet guy who drives in 100 runs every year," said Gillick. "The kind of guy you win titles with." Toronto's other key players were Gold Glove center fielder Devon White, catcher Pat Borders, and Ed Sprague, who had taken over as the team's third baseman.

While the Jays could hit with any team, they were thin on the mound. Juan Guzman, the acknowledged ace of the staff, had had his season interrupted by injury. But he did compile a 14–3 record, and showed a strong finishing kick by going undefeated after July 7. Stewart had also finished strongly, but his 12–8 record showed that at 37 years of age, he wasn't the same pitcher who had regularly reeled off 20-win seasons for the A's. The pitcher who had kept the staff glued together was the unheralded Pat Hentgen, who had surprised everyone by winning 19 games in his first season as a regular. But when manager Cito Gaston sent out Todd Stottlemyre, or tried to use someone else in a starter's role, it was as risky as trying to ice skate on melting ice.

In the bullpen, the Jays used a varied cast of set-up men and middle relievers. But the main man was closer Tom Henke, who had tied for the league lead in saves with 45. Gillick was well aware of the fact that the pitching staff could turn out to be Toronto's Achilles' heel. "Offensively and defensively we have a better team than last year's model. But from a pitching depth standpoint, we're not as good as last year."

The White Sox, on the other hand, were pitching rich, starting with Cy Young award-winner Jack McDowell who had led the AL with 22 wins. Close behind Black Jack were 18-game winner Alex Fernandez, 15-game winner Wilson Alvarez, and rookie Jason Bere, who had reeled off seven straight wins to finish the season at 12–5.

Sammy Ellis, the Seattle Mariners' pitching coach, joined a large chorus of experts when he called the Chisox starters the top quartet in the AL. "They're aggressive and go after you with good hard fastballs, good hard breaking balls and just challenge you to hit them."

Scott Redinsky was the workhorse in the bullpen

with 73 appearances, but Roberto Hernandez was the thoroughbred, with a 2.29 ERA and 38 saves.

Offensively, the Sox were led by the 1993 AL MVP, Frank Thomas. The Big Hurt had compiled a .317 average and his booming bat had hammered out 41 home runs and knocked in 128 runs. The Sox also relied on outfielders Lance Johnson and Tim Raines, both of whom had hit over .300, as well as third baseman Robin Ventura, who had cracked 22 round-trippers while driving in 94 runs. And while designated hitters George Bell, who hit only .217, and Bo Jackson, who wasn't much better at .232, had turned in disappointing batting averages, they had combined to swat 29 dingers and collect 109 RBI.

The Jays figured to have the advantage of post-season experience on their side. At least Joe Carter was counting on that edge. "Hopefully, the Chicago players will be a little bit nervous with this being their first time in the playoffs."

But the key factor in the American League Championship Series figured to turn on whether or not the Chisox pitchers could slow down the nonstop Jays offense, which included five players—White, Alomar, Henderson, Olerud, and Molitor—who had each scored over 100 runs, and three players—Molitor, Olerud, and Carter—who had each racked up more than 100 RBI.

"This is a very intimidating lineup," declared Carter. "If I was pitching, I'd be intimidated by us. A pitcher doesn't have a chance to relax against us. One guy you might want to relax against, Pat Borders, was the World Series MVP last year. The other guy, Ed Sprague, had 73 RBI. If you're a pitcher, you've got to be mentally sharp, because we're not going to give you a break."

The Jays gave the Chisox a letter-perfect demonstration of what Carter meant in the first game of the ALCS, as they mauled McDowell for 13 hits and six runs on their way to a 7–3 win at Chicago's Comisky Park. Molitor, with four hits, including a home run, and three RBI was a one-man wrecking crew, while Ed Sprague and John Olerud combined for seven hits and split four RBI. And although Juan Guzman wasn't as sharp as he usually was, he was as tough as he had to be, while relievers Danny Cox and Duane Ward shut the Sox down over the final three innings.

The citizens of the Windy City absorbed more than their fair quota of bad news the following morning when Michael Jordan, who had led the Chicago Bulls to three straight NBA championships, stunned the sports world by announcing that he was hanging up his Nikes and retiring from professional basketball.

And life wasn't about to get any easier for Chicagoans, because later in the day the Sox had to face Dave Stewart, the winningest pitcher in ALCS history with a 6–0 mark. "He's just cocky this time of year," said Carter. "He practically guarantees you a victory."

Stewart lived up to his press clippings by limiting the Sox to one run over six innings and then Al Leiter and Duane Ward, who picked up his second save of the series, protected the Jays' 3–1 win. Stewart showed what he was all about in the sixth inning by pitching out of a bases-loaded, no-out jam. "Throughout my career, in the ALCS, something different happens," said Stewart, who had struggled though a mediocre season while posting a 4.44 ERA. "I can't explain it, but I'm going to ride it for as long as I can."

Although the Sox had tied an ALCS record for futility by stranding 23 base runners in the first two games, the Jays weren't about to be lulled into complacency. "We're not going to get into a situation where we're calling the White Sox dead," said Molitor, who had set an ALCS record of his own by striking six straight hits over the two games. "Too many strange things can happen."

Although the next three games were scheduled in Toronto, Jays manager Cito Gaston, knowing that Chicago had compiled the best road record in the AL, echoed Molitor's concern. "I'm sure the White Sox aren't feeling too good, but baseball is a funny game. It can turn on you."

Which is exactly what happened over the next two games as the Sox evened the series by taking two straight at the SkyDome. Wilson Alvarez, who had finished the season with seven straight victories, continued on his winning ways with a 6–1 complete game gem against Pat Hentgen.

In the next game, the Jays should have known it wasn't going to be their day in the second inning, when Lance Johnson jumped all over a Todd Stottlemyre pitch and sent it sailing over the right-field fence. The

2-run blast was the first round-tripper for Johnson in 689 at-bats, dating back to August 24, 1992. "We've been on Lance all season about that," said Frank Thomas. "But I guess he waited for the right time to finally hit one."

The Jays battled back against Jason Bere in the bottom of the third as they rallied for three runs on an RBI single by Alomar and a 2-run single by Carter. But then the Sox took the lead for good as they struck for three runs in the sixth.

The Big Hurt started the bashing by crashing his big bat into a Stottlemyre fastball that landed with a thud in the second deck. One out later, Stottlemyre got himself into more trouble by walking Ellis Burks and Bo Jackson. Johnson once again made him pay the price by lashing a 2-run triple to the base of the center-field wall that gave the Sox a 5–3 lead. "He hadn't made any mistakes against me all year," said Johnson, who had been 0–7 against Stottlemyre during the regular season. "But he made two tonight. Same pitch, both times. Both fastballs. Put 'em right up where I like 'em."

Although the Jays cut the score to 5–4 in their half of the sixth on an RBI double by Alomar, the Sox added single runs in the seventh and ninth to tie the series at 2–2.

The Chicago win marked the first time that the visiting teams had won the first four games of an ALCS, and Jack McDowell and his White Sox teammates were hoping to extend that streak for one more game. But McDowell didn't rise to the occasion, as he surrendered single runs in each of the three innings that he pitched. The Jays added a fourth run on an RBI double by Alomar, who also swiped three bases, and then closed out their scoring in the seventh on Sprague's second RBI of the game.

Juan Guzman, meanwhile, was overpowering, as he retired the first 13 batters he faced before Ellis Burks snapped the string by belting a home run in the top of the fifth inning. The Sox then cut the gap to 5–3 when Robin Ventura whacked a 2-run homer off Ward in the ninth. And Ward dug the hole a little deeper when he plucked Burks with a pitch, which brought Bo Jackson to the plate with a chance to tie the game. But Ward climbed up out of the ditch by whiffing Bo and giving the Jays a 3-games-to-2 lead.

While the teams trekked back to Chicago, Dave Stewart, Toronto's starting pitcher in Game 6, stayed behind to fulfill some plans he had made before the ALCS had started. Thanksgiving Day in Canada falls in October, and Stewart had previously committed himself to sponsoring and serving a Thanksgiving Day meal in a Toronto homeless center. "I've been community-oriented ever since I got into baseball," said Stewart, who had hosted similar dinners in Oakland during his years with the A's. "This is Canada, but I haven't noticed any difference at all; people are people.

"To me, there are people out there, deserving people, who have had bad breaks. It would be a selfish thing to make all the money I do and not give something back to the community."

The extra work didn't take anything away from Stewart, as he held the Jays to two runs in a 7⅓ inning stint the following night. And neither did the weather in Chicago, which was so cold that Stew couldn't grip the ball well enough to throw breaking pitches. So Stewart, who was named the Series MVP, had to tough it out with only his fastball and his courage, while upping his ALCS record to 8–0.

The Jays opened the scoring in the second inning on a 2-run double by Borders. That was a bad omen for the Sox, since the team that scored first had won the previous five games.

Although the Sox tied the game in the following inning, the Jays retook the lead, 3–2, when they nicked Alex Fernandez for an unearned run in the top of the fourth. That was all the scoring until the top of the ninth when Devon White took Radinsky downtown and Molitor lined a 2-run triple that upped the Jays lead to 6–2. A solo home run by Warren Newson in the bottom of the ninth cut Toronto's lead to 6–3, but Ward retired the Sox without any further damage as the Jays captured their second consecutive pennant. "That's all we wanted," said Ward. "A chance to go back to the World Series and defend our title."

Atlanta, which had won two consecutive National League pennants, was the preseason pick to go all the way in 1993 and win the World Series. The team had fortified its already formidable starting pitching staff by signing free agent Greg Maddux, the 1992 Cy Young award-winner. Maddux had lived up to his star billing and big salary by turning in a 2.36 ERA, tops among Major League starters, while winning 20 games and earning his second consecutive Cy Young award.

Atlanta had another pair of aces in Tom Glavine, the 1991 Cy Young award-winner who had led the NL with 22 wins, his third consecutive 20-win season; and 18-game winner Steve Avery. Altanta's fourth starter was John Smoltz, a big-game pitcher who owned a 5–0 record in postseason play.

Altanta also featured the power-hitting duo of right fielder David Justice, whose 40 home runs and 120 RBI were second only to Barry Bonds among NL sluggers; and left fielder Ron Gant, who popped 37 round-trippers and drove in 117 runs.

But with all that pitching and all that power, Atlanta still trailed the Bobby Bonds–led San Francisco Giants by 10 games during the third week of July. During that same week, however, Atanta acquired slugging first baseman Fred McGriff in a lopsided swap with the San Diego Padres. The trade for McGriff lit up the Atlanta team, which went on to win 50 of their final 68 games. "He made everybody feel we could win every game," said Atlanta manager Bobby Cox.

But even with the addition of McGriff, who finished the season with 37 home runs and 101 RBI, Atlanta didn't wrap up the division until the final day of the season when they knocked off the Colorado Rockies, and the Giants were demolished 12–1 by the Los Angeles Dodgers. For the Dodgers, it was a payback for

1991, when the Giants had knocked them out of the playoff picture on the next-to-last day of the season.

It was also the latest installment in a long-standing rivalry that dates back to the days when both the Dodgers and the Giants played in New York City. "We love to beat the Giants," boomed Dodgers manager Tommy Lasorda. "Not just today, but all the time."

The Phillies' rocket ride to the top of the NL East was sparked by the high octane play of its scrappy center fielder, Lenny Dykstra. The left-handed-hitting human sparkplug had led the majors with 143 runs scored, and was the NL pacesetter in hits and walks, becoming only the third player in baseball history to lead a league in hits, walks, and runs scored. "He's the catalyst," said Phils manager Jim Fregosi. "He's the reason we score as many runs as we do."

And no other team in the Senior Circuit had crossed the plate as often as the Phils, who did it 877 times, 69 more than the runner-up Giants and 110 ahead of Atlanta.

In addition to Dykstra, the Phils received prime-time numbers from first baseman John Kruk, who hit for a .316 average; catcher Darren Daulton, who led the team with 105 RBI; and third baseman Dave Hollins, who drove in 93 runs. The Phil's engine was also propelled by the outstanding production of their left-field platoon of Pete Incaviglia and Milt Thomson, who combined for 27 home runs, 119 RBI, and a .270 batting average. The platoon system worked for the Phils in right field, too, where Jim Eisenreich and Wes Chamberlain produced 19 dingers, drove in 95 runs and hit for a .306 batting average.

And the Phils received another big boost from second baseman Mariano Duncan, who drove in 73 runs, and rookie Kevin Stocker, a midseason call-up who had plugged a hole at shortstop and surprised everybody by stroking the ball at a .324 clip.

Collectively, the Phils, in addition to leading the league in runs scored, had also finished first in doubles, extra-base hits, walks, and on-base percentage. "Every time you look at them, they have two guys on base," said White Sox scout Eddie Brinkman.

The Phils also had two very hot right-handed pitchers, Tommy Greene and Curt Schilling, who finished at 16–4 and 16–7, respectively, while dropping only one game each after the All-Star Game. The big question marks among the starting staff were the two left-handers: Danny Jackson, who had a mediocre 12–11 record; and Terry Mulholland, who wound up at 12–9 and had only pitched 5 innings since injuring a hip muscle on September 6.

The bullpen was another area of concern for the Phils because their relievers had compiled a 4.05 ERA, nearly a run higher than their Atlanta counterparts. And while Mitch Williams, the "Wild Thing," had saved 43 games and blown only six, his lack of control and his propensity for giving up hits had made his every appearance a tension-filled high-wire act.

Although the Phils had the scoring stats on their side and had split their 12 regular season games with

Atlanta, Atlanta was still considered the odds-on favorite to pop the Phils' bubble.

The Phillies, though, were used to being under-dogs, and actually seemed to delight in their image as a collection of oddballs and long-haired, big-bellied out-casts. "We got written off in spring training," laughed John Kruk. "We were supposed to finish behind the Florida Marlins—an expansion team!"

And while the Phils expressed great respect for Atlanta, to a man they seemed to have adopted the motto that Mitch Williams had inscribed on his head-band: "NO FEAR."

The first game of the NLCS gave the Phils fans who packed Veterans Stadium everything they had come to both fear and love about their hometown team.

Dykstra, naturally, set the tone by lashing a first-inning double off Steve Avery and then coming in to score the initial run of the series on a groundout by Kruk. Curt Schilling, meanwhile, was putting on a pitching clinic performance, setting an LCS record by striking out the first five Atlanta hitters that he faced. Schilling finished his eight-inning stint with 10 K's, and yielded only two runs, one of which was tainted by two consecutive fly balls that were misplayed into doubles by Incaviglia in left field. Inky, though, made up for his gaffes with one swing of his bat, and after Avery had wild-pitched home another run, the Phils took a 3–2 lead into the ninth inning.

But Williams, as a matter of course, walked the first batter he faced. "It's just Mitch. What can you do?"

shrugged Kruk afterwards. "Guys get on base, they say to me, 'I couldn't take this if he was on my team.' But I've got calluses built on my heart."

That free pass quickly turned into the tying run, helped along by a two-base throwing error by third baseman Kim Batiste, who, ironically, had just been put into the game as a defensive replacement for Dave Hollins.

Williams also caused the Phils fans to hold their breath in the tenth inning by giving up consecutive two-out base hits before he powered his way out of the jam by striking out pinch-hitter Tony Tarasco.

The Phils, though, finally sent their fans home shaking but smiling when, in the bottom of the tenth, Kruk doubled to right off Greg McMichael, and then Batiste, the would-be goat of the game, became its hero by bouncing a single down the third-base line that sent Kruk lumbering home with the winning run. For some teams, the game would look like one of those sequels to *Friday the 13th*, but to the Phils, it was just another day at the office.

The Phils were looking to sweep the two-game set at the Vet behind Tommy Greene, who had posted a perfect 10–0 record in 16 home starts during the regular season. But Fred McGriff started to squash that notion in the first inning when he launched a massive home run into the upper deck in right field. Two innings later, Atlanta batters treated Greene as if he were a batting-practice pitcher by scorching him for six runs. Shortstop Jeff Blauser started the barrage with a home run. And after two hits and a walk loaded the bases, Terry Pendleton stroked a 2-run single to right that ended Greene's brief outing. Bobby Thigpen came in to put out the fire, but instead poured oil on the blaze by serving up a 3-run homer to catcher Damon Berryhill.

Before the game was over, Atlanta had pummelled Phils pitching for an LCS-record 14 runs, while Greg Maddux and a pair of relievers were limiting the Phils to three runs on a 2-run homer by Hollins and a solo shot by Dykstra.

"It wasn't pretty," admitted Phils manager Jim Fregosi. "You get balls out over the plate for them to hit, they're going to hit them."

The scene shifted to Atlanta–Fulton County Stadium for Game 3, with Terry Mulholland matched against Tom Glavine. The Phils grabbed the upper hand early in the game as Kruk rocked Glavine for a run-scoring triple in the fourth inning and a solo homer in the top of the sixth, while Mulholland cruised through the first five innings. But in the bottom of the sixth the Atlanta attack got itself untracked and sank Mulholland with a 5-run inning. Once again, Blauser started the rally with an infield single and David Justice capped it off with a 2-run double. Atlanta then put the game away with a 4-run seventh inning that featured a 3-run double by second baseman Mark Lemke.

"Our pitching has been a little shaky the last two games, but our offense hasn't been too darned good either. But other than that, we're in good shape," snapped Kruk.

Winning pitcher Tom Glavine tried to give his team an extra edge by playing a little mind game on Danny Jackson, the Phils' starting pitcher in the fourth game. "If I was in his place and had seen 23 runs scored in two games, I might be wondering, 'How am I going to stop these guys?' " ·

Jackson, though, turned a deaf ear to Glavine's ploy as he limited Atlanta to one run in 7⅔ innings, while the Phils were coaxing two unearned runs off John Smoltz. Williams, who entered the game with two outs in the eighth, closed it out without allowing a score and the series was tied 2–2.

Game 5 looked like a lock for the Phils, as Curt Schilling, with the help of some great outfield defense, took a 3–0 lead into the ninth inning. But Schilling committed a basic pitching no-no by walking the leadoff hitter, Jeff Blauser. After another Kim Batiste error allowed Ron Gant to reach base, Schilling was out and Williams was in. And the game was about to take a walk on the wild side.

McGriff greeted Williams with an RBI single that sent Gant galloping into third. Justice followed with a sac fly that shaved the Phils lead to 3–2, and Pendleton kept the rally going by moving McGriff to second with a single. Then pinch-hitter Franciso Caberra, who had delivered the pennant-winning hit for Atlanta a year earlier, singled in McGriff with the tying run as Pendleton trucked around to third.

"It was slipping away," recalled Dykstra afterward. "Everyone felt it. You just wanted to be able to call a time-out, like in basketball." But with the winning run only 90 feet and one wild pitch away from breaking the Phils' spirit, Williams sent the game into extra innings by whiffing Mark Lemke and getting pinch-hitter Bill Pecota on a harmless fly to center.

Williams had given Dykstra his time-out and in the top of the tenth Dykstra, the player whom the Phillies call the Dude, drilled a Mark Wohlers pitch over the fence in right-center to give the Phils a 4–3 lead. "It's been like that all year," said Fregosi. "The guys on this team look to Lenny to do something. And when they do, he finds a way to get it done."

Atlanta had a last chance to turn the game back in their direction, but veteran reliever Larry Anderson set them down in the bottom of the tenth to nail down the Phils' win.

Although the Phils now led the series 3–2, and only needed to win one of the two games back at Vets Stadium, they knew they still had a hard road to travel. "They've got Madddux and Glavine lined up," said Dykstra, who remembered that Atlanta had been in this same fix in 1991 and had won back-to-back shutouts to snatch the pennant away from the Pittsburgh Pirates. "We're happy and excited, but we still have to win one more. There's no reason to win three if you don't win four."

Darren Daulton got the Phils moving in that right direction in the third inning of game six, when he touched Maddux for a 2-out, 2-run double. The fifth inning, though, was the real turning point of the game.

In the top of the frame, Atlanta had already scored once and had two other runners in scoring position when Tommy Greene caught Ron Gant looking at a third strike to retire the side and preserve the Phils one-run edge. And then, in the bottom of the fifth, Dave Hollins drilled a no-doubt-about-it 2-run homer over the center-field fence to give the Phils a 4–1 lead.

One inning later, second baseman Mickey Morandini hooked a 2-run triple into the right-field corner which offset a too- little-too-late 2-run homer by Jeff Blauser in the top of the seventh. Then David West, who pitched a perfect eighth inning and Mitch Williams, who set the side down in order in the ninth, preserved the 6–3 win that earned the Phils the 1993 NL pennant. "Only three guys came to the plate, I don't know what happened," laughed Wild Thing.

It had been a strange series, with the losing team outhitting the winning team by .274 to .227 and outscoring them by 10 runs. Some of the Atlanta players, like Terry Pendleton, were gracious in defeat. "People will be looking for reasons why we lost. The reason is in the other clubhouse." But most of the media experts and a lot of the Atlanta players weren't ready to accept the fact that the best team had won. "They beat us and we have to give them credit, but I still think we're a better team," said Greg Maddux, who had lost the deciding game for a team that was earning the reputation of being the Buffalo Bills of baseball.

The Phils, though, had fed off that type of disrespect throughout the season and now they were headed to the World Series. "We were picked to be a last-place team and this team loves to prove people wrong," said Mitch Williams. "We're a bunch of castoffs and we have one goal: To show everybody who ever got rid of us and said we couldn't play."

The World Series opened in the SkyDome with the teams' top aces, Juan Guzman and Curt Schilling, taking the mound, but before the game was over, Roberto Alomar would show just why he's considered to be the king of major league second basemen.

The Phils jumped out to a first-inning lead as Dykstra the Igniter drew a leadoff walk, stole second and then raced home on Kruk's single to left field. And after a walk to Hollins, Daulton's single to center scored Kruk with the Phils' second run of the inning.

The Jays knotted the score in the bottom of the second on an RBI single by Molitor and a run-scoring groundout by Tony Fernandez. The Phils, though, recaptured the lead in the bottom of the third as Duncan delivered a leadoff single, swiped second and then motored home on Kruk's base hit.

The Jays, playing follow-the-leader again, tied the score at 3–3 in their next turn at bat on a sac fly by Joe Carter. Then, in the top of the fifth, the visitors inched ahead one last time, 4–3, and only a Play-of-the-Day catch by Alomar on a soft drive by Dykstra prevented the Phillies from pulling even further ahead. Dykstra's little flair over first base looked like a sure base hit, but Alomar, racing back and to his left, made a spectacular diving catch while sliding across the foul line. The play saved at least one run for sure when Mariano Duncan followed with a three-bagger off the top of the left-field wall. Although Duncan scored on a wild pitch by Guzman, the Jays felt fortunate to be trailing by only a single run. Then, in the top of the fifth, Toronto tied the game for the third and last time with one blast off of Devon White's bat.

The never-say-die Phils made a bid to retake the lead in the top of the sixth when, with two-out and runners on first and second, Duncan drilled a single up the middle past reliever Al Leiter. But Alomar, ranging far to his right this time, knocked the ball down and kept Kevin Stocker from scoring the go-ahead run. "He played me the other way, and he still got it," marveled Duncan. "That's what makes him the best second baseman in the majors. He takes care of the whole right side of their infield."

Then Leiter, a former Yankee phenom, who has had a mostly disappointing and injury-plagued career, made Alomar's second POD worth the effort by smoking a third strike past Kruk. "That was a little nerve-wracking, but I really went after it," said a smiling Leiter.

The Jays finally moved into the lead, 5–4, when Olerud smoked a solo home run just inside the right-field foul pole. Then they broke the game open with a three-run seventh inning that was capped by Alomar's 2-run double off of David West.

"This team has a lot of heart," noted Toronto manager Cito Gaston following the Jays' 8–5 win. "They play hard and they don't quit."

Gaston gave the ball to Stewart for Game 2, hoping that the veteran right-hander would give the Jays a sweep of the two-game set at the SkyDome. But the Phils spoiled that strategy by scorching Stewart for five runs in the third inning, more than he had ever surrendered in any postseason game. Dykstra, as usual, lit the fuse, but Jim Eisenreich supplied the fireworks by blasting a 3-run homer over the right-center field fence.

The home run was the crowning moment for the 34-year-old outfielder who had missed the better part of five seasons while he battled Tourette's Syndrome, an illness that causes people to sometimes jerk their bodies and shout uncontrollably. Although some unthinking dolts still try to distract Eisenreich by cruelly mimicking him, he just shrugs. "It doesn't bother me. I'm on the field. They're not."

The Jays, though, fought back and sliced the Phils' lead to 5–2 when Molitor opened the fourth inning with a single and Carter took Mulholland downtown. And then they closed to 5–3 on a two-out RBI double by Fernandez that knocked Mulholland out of the game.

Dykstra, though, changed the shifting momentum of the game back in the Phils' direction by drilling a leadoff homer in the top of the seventh that upped their lead to 6–3. And after the Jays had narrowed the gap with a run in the eighth, Mitch Williams came in to shut the door and save the Phils' 6–4 win.

In gaining a split at the SkyDome, the Phils had

taken the home field advantage away from the Jays. And with the Series moving to Philadelphia for the next three games, the teams would be forced, by baseball's strange rules, to play without a designated hitter. That changeover didn't create any problems for Jim Fregosi, since NL teams don't use a designated during the season or in the NLCS. But the situation did pose a king-sized dilemma for Cito Gaston.

He could sit Molitor, who had posted the league's second highest batting average and was the team's hottest hitter over the second half of the season. Or he could bench John Olerud, the AL's top hitter, and use Molitor at first base, where he had played only 23 times during the past season. Gaston's final option was to sit Ed Sprague and put Molitor at the hot corner. But playing Molitor at third base would potentially weaken Toronto defensively, since he hadn't played there for three years, and it would also heighten the risk of injury to his already tender right shoulder.

Gaston's tough decision was made a lot easier by the fact that all three players had their eyes focused on the prize of the World Series and were willing to put the team's welfare ahead of their own individual ambitions. "I have a great deal of respect for what it means to win a world championship, and I'll do anything Cito asks me to do to help us win," said Molitor, who had been to the Big Dance only once in his 15 years with the Brewers. And both Sprague and Olerud voiced similar sentiments.

Gaston finally opted to sit the left-handed hitting

Olerud, and let the right-handed hitting Molitor take his cuts against the southpaw offerings of Danny Jackson.

Molitor made Gaston look like a certified genius by igniting a 3-run first-inning outburst with a 2-run triple. And two innings later, Molitor muscled a two-out homer over the left-field fence to move the Jays out to a 4–0 lead and give Pat Hengsten all the support he would need. Toronto, though, added another run in the sixth, as Alomar opened the inning with a single and then proceeded to steal second and third before crossing the plate on a sac fly by Fernandez. And Toronto continued to pummel the Phils by adding three runs in the seventh and another pair in the ninth to win going away, 10–3.

Molitor had had a big day at the plate and while he showed some rust in the field, he also started a 3-6-1 double play that snuffed out a Phils rally. "I wasn't coordinated at times, but getting off to a good start offensively made it easier to play defense," said Molitor, who wound up playing the next two games at third base.

Game 4 should have come with instructions for fans to buckle their seat belts, because they were about to witness one of the wildest games in World Series history. The tone for the game was set in the first inning, when Toronto touched Tommy Greene for three runs, and the Phils responded by shelling Todd Stottlemyre for four runs, including a 3-run triple by Milt Thompson.

The Phils tacked on two more runs in the second

inning as Greene, doing better with his bat than his arm, singled and then walked home as Dykstra followed by ripping a home run down the right-field line to up their lead to 6–3. But the Jays bounced back in the top of the third, by bruising the Phils for four runs as they took a 7–6 lead and sent Greene to an early and well-deserved shower.

The Phils, though, evened the score in the fourth inning as Dykstra drilled a 2-out double to right-center and then rode home on Duncan's clutch hit. And then in the fifth inning, the Phils finally seemed to ice the game when they lit up Al Leiter for five runs and moved out to a 12–7 lead. Daulton started the onslaught with a 2-run homer and Dykstra ended it with another 2-run dinger. That blast brought the hometown fans out of their seats, while the Philly Phanatic, the team's mascot, did a taunting dance in front of the Toronto dugout.

Even after the Jays cut the Phils' lead with two runs in the top of the sixth, the Phils answered right back with a run in the bottom of the sixth and another in the seventh to take a 14–9 lead into the eighth inning. At this point even some of the Jays were ready to concede defeat. "When they got that lead up to five runs again, I thought, 'We'll get 'em tomorrow,'" admitted Devon White.

But the Jays only waited until their next turn at bat. Then they battered a trio of Phillies pitchers for six runs, including a 2-run triple by Devon White that gave the Jays the lead and the game, 15–14. "This game will be remembered forever in baseball history," said Dave

Stewart, who had watched it from the safety of the Jays' dugout. "But I don't think anybody will deny that from a pitcher's standpoint, it was an ugly, ugly game."

It was also a game that set a slew of records including the most runs ever scored in a postseason game, shattering the previous mark of 22 that had stood since Game 2 of the 1936 Series when the Yankees clobbered the New York Giants, 18–4. "It was like a slow-pitch softball game out there," chuckled Joe Carter.

And it was a heartbreaking game for the Philadelphia players. "I just couldn't get them out," said a bleary-eyed Mitch Williams, who had given up the last 3 runs of the game. "No whining, no crying, no excuses. I was just trying to make pitches and I couldn't do it. Sometimes your arm just doesn't have any life in it."

"There's not much I can say to describe my feelings," added Dykstra, who had homered twice, doubled and scored a Series record-tying four runs. "Everyone knows we let it get away. You don't have to be a baseball genius to figure that out. But this one is over and we still have tomorrow."

With the Phils trailing three games to one and facing elimination, Curt Schilling, who had been hit hard in Game 1, was the man in charge of keeping alive the Phillies' faint hopes. "I had too many plans in the first game," explained Schilling, who had dutifully studied tapes of the Toronto hitters. "This time I won't worry about trying to pitch to their weaknesses, I'll pitch to my strengths."

Schilling talked the talk and then he went out and

walked the walk as he shut out the Jays, 2–0. After the record-shattering slugfest of Game 4, it was a case of going from the ridiculous to the sublime.

Schilling got all the help he needed in the first inning when—who else?—Dykstra, after drawing a walk from Guzman, stole second, continued on to third when Pat Borders' throw sailed into center field and then came in to score on Kruk's groundout. The Phils, though, added an insurance run in the second inning when Kevin Stocker stroked a clutch 2-out double that drove in Darren Daulton.

Juan Guzman, who pitched well enough to win most games, kept waiting for the cavalry to arrive, but the Jays offense, which had averaged just over nine runs per game in the previous four games, never mounted a charge.

Game 6, like Game 4, turned into an emotional roller-coaster ride for players and fans alike.

The Jays bats, which had slumbered through the previous game, received an early wake-up call and staked Stewart to a 3–0 first-inning lead. Molitor got the action started by tripling home White who had drawn a one-out walk from Mulholland. Carter's sac fly brought in Molitor with the second run, and after Olerud drilled a 2-out double into the gap in left-center, Alomar picked him up with a line single to center.

The Phils, after being held hitless for 3⅔ innings by Stewart, finally bunched two of them together and trimmed their deficit to 3–1 as Daulton drove a double to deep left field and came in to score on Eisenriech's single to center. But the Jays made the Phils feel like they were just standing on a treadmill by answering back with a run of their own in the bottom of the fourth.

The outlook for the Phils turned even bleaker in the fifth inning, as Stewart pitched his way out of a bases-loaded jam in the top half of the inning, and then Molitor hammered a home run in the bottom of the frame to raise the Jays' lead to 5–1.

Stewart, who was still working on a 2-hitter, sailed into the seventh inning without a cloud on the horizon. But then he committed a pitching bugaboo by issuing a leadoff walk to Stocker. And after Mickey Morandini followed with a single, Dykstra drilled a 3-run home run that sliced the Jays' lead to 5–4, and knocked Stewart out of the game.

Danny Cox was brought into the game to contain the rally, but Duncan kept it going with a single and a swipe of second. And after Cox struck out Kruk, Hollins stroked a single that drove in Duncan with the tying run. After Daulton kept the rally alive by drawing a walk, and Eisenreich legged out an infield single, Gaston brought in Leiter to put on the breaks. But Fregosi countered by sending Incaviglia up to pinch hit and Inky came through with a sacrifice fly that put the Phils in front, 6–5.

The Phils took that razor-thin margin into the ninth inning and gave the ball to Mitch Williams to protect the lead and force a seventh game. But Wild Thing started off on a sour note by issuing an inning-opening base-on-balls to Rickey Henderson. Williams brought the Phils one step closer to a win when he got White to fly out, but Molitor's single moved Henderson into scoring position. And then Joe Carter shot a bolt of electricity through the SkyDome by lining a 3-run home run over the left-field fence that gave the Jays an 8–6 win and made them the first team to repeat as World Series champions since the New York Yankees won back-to-back titles in 1977–78.

As Carter circled the bases, jumping up and down in a dance of joy, Lenny Dykstra sagged with the sadness of defeat. "It was a weird feeling seeing that ball fly out," said Dykstra, who had played with the skills and the heart of a champion. "I felt helpless. But we never quit and we never died. We showed everybody that we have character and we have courage."

And while lots of the Philadelphia fans turned on Williams, his teammates kept his blown saves in the proper perspective. "What people tend to forget is that, without Mitch, we're not here," said John Kruk. "People can say what they want about him, but we're not blaming him for anything."

Over in the winners' clubhouse, Paul Molitor, who had hit .500 and was named the World Series MVP, was feeling a quiet satisfaction about being on a World Series-winning team for the first time in his 16-year career. "Yes, I'm excited. But there's something peaceful about accomplishing what you set out to do. This definitely is something that in the days and weeks ahead will grow deeper and deeper in appreciation."

WORLD SERIES RESULTS

1903 Boston AL 5, Pittsburgh NL 3
1904 No series
1905 New York NL 4, Philadelphia AL 1
1906 Chicago AL 4, Chicago NL 2
1907 Chicago NL 4, Detroit AL 0, 1 tie
1908 Chicago NL 4, Detroit AL 1
1909 Pittsburgh NL 4, Detroit AL 3
1910 Philadelphia AL 4, Chicago NL 1
1911 Philadelphia AL 4, New York NL 2
1912 Boston AL 4, New York NL 3, 1 tie
1913 Philadelphia AL 4, New York NL 1
1914 Boston NL 4, Philadelphia AL 0
1915 Boston AL 4, Philadelphia NL 1
1916 Boston AL 4, Brooklyn NL 1
1917 Chicago AL 4, New York NL 2
1918 Boston AL 4, Chicago NL 2
1919 Cincinnati NL 5, Chicago AL 3
1920 Cleveland AL 5, Brooklyn NL 2
1921 New York NL 5, New York AL 3
1922 New York NL 4, New York AL 0, 1 tie
1923 New York AL 4, New York NL 2
1924 Washington AL 4, New York NL 3
1925 Pittsburgh NL 4, Washington AL 3
1926 St. Louis NL 4, New York AL 3
1927 New York AL 4, Pittsburgh NL 0
1928 New York AL 4, St. Louis NL 0
1929 Philadelphia AL 4, Chicago NL 1
1930 Philadelphia AL 4, St. Louis NL 2
1931 St. Louis NL 4, Philadelphia AL 3
1932 New York AL 4, Chicago NL 0
1933 New York NL 4, Washington AL 1
1934 St. Louis Nl 4, Detroit AL 3
1935 Detroit AL 4, Chicago NL 2
1936 New York AL 4, New York NL 2
1937 New York AL 4, New York NL 1
1938 New York AL 4, Chicago NL 0
1939 New York AL 4, Cincinnati NL 0
1940 Cincinnati NL 4, Detroit AL 3
1941 New York AL 4, Brooklyn NL 1
1942 St. Louis NL 4, New York AL 1
1943 New York AL 4, St. Louis NL 1
1944 St. Louis NL 4, St. Louis AL 2
1945 Detroit AL 4, Chicago NL 3
1946 St. Louis NL 4, Boston AL 3
1947 New York AL 4, Brooklyn NL 3

1948 Cleveland AL 4, Boston NL 2
1949 New York AL 4, Brooklyn NL 1
1950 New York AL 4, Philadelphia NL 0
1951 New York AL 4, New York NL 2
1952 New York AL 4, Brooklyn NL 3
1953 New York AL 4, Brooklyn NL 2
1954 New York NL 4, Cleveland AL 0
1955 Brooklyn NL 4, New York AL 3
1956 New York AL 4, Brooklyn NL 3
1957 Milwaukee NL 4, New York AL 3
1958 New York AL 4, Milwaukee NL 3
1959 Los Angeles NL 4, Chicago AL 2
1960 Pittsburgh NL 4, New York AL 3
1961 New York AL 4, Cincinnati NL 1
1962 New York AL 4, San Francisco NL 3
1963 Los Angeles NL 4, New York AL 0
1964 St. Louis NL 4, New York AL 3
1965 Los Angeles NL 4, Minnesota AL 3
1966 Baltimore AL 4, Los Angeles NL 0
1967 St. Louis NL 4, Boston AL 3
1968 Detroit AL 4, St. Louis NL 3
1969 New York NL 4, Baltimore AL 1
1970 Baltimore AL 4, Cincinnati NL 1
1971 Pittsburgh NL 4, Baltimore AL 3
1972 Oakland AL 4, Cincinnati NL 3
1973 Oakland AL 4, New York NL 3
1974 Oakland AL 4, Los Angeles NL 1
1975 Cincinnati NL 4, Boston AL 3
1976 Cincinnati NL 4, New York AL 0
1977 New York AL 4, Los Angeles NL 2
1978 New York AL 4, Los Angeles NL 2
1979 Pittsburgh NL 4, Baltimore AL 3
1980 Philadelphia NL 4, Kansas City AL 2
1981 Los Angeles NL 4, New York AL 2
1982 St. Louis NL 4, Milwaukee AL 3
1983 Baltimore AL 4, Philadelphia NL 1
1984 Detroit AL 4, San Diego NL 1
1985 Kansas City AL 4, St. Louis NL 3
1986 New York NL 4, Boston AL 3
1987 Minnesota AL 4, St. Louis NL 3
1988 Los Angeles NL 4, Oakland AL 1
1989 Oakland AL 4, San Francisco NL 0
1990 Cincinnati NL 4, Oakland AL 0
1991 Minnesota AL 4, Atlanta NL 3
1992 Toronto AL 4, Atlanta NL 2
1993 Toronto AL 4, Philadelphia NL 2

WORLD SERIES MVPS

1955 Johnny Podres, Brooklyn (NL)
1956 Don Larsen, New York (AL)
1957 Lew Burdette, Milwaukee (NL)
1958 Bob Turley, New York (AL)
1959 Larry Sherry, Los Angeles (NL)
1960 Bobby Richardson, New York (AL)
1961 Whitey Ford, New York (AL)
1962 Ralph Terry, New York (AL)
1963 Sandy Koufax, Los Angeles (NL)
1964 Bob Gibson, St. Louis (NL)
1965 Sandy Koufax, Los Angeles (NL)
1966 Frank Robinson, Baltimore (AL)
1967 Bob Gibson, St. Louis (NL)
1968 Mickey Lolich, Detroit (AL)
1969 Donn Clendenon, New York (NL)
1970 Brooks Robinson, Baltimore (AL)
1971 Roberto Clemente, Pittsburgh (NL)
1972 Gene Tenace, Oakland (AL)
1973 Reggie Jackson, Oakland (AL)
1974 Rollie Fingers, Oakland (AL)

1975 Pete Rose, Cincinnati (NL)
1976 Johnny Bench, Cincinnati (NL)
1977 Reggie Jackson, New York (AL)
1978 Bucky Dent, New York (AL)
1979 Willie Stargell, Pittsburgh (NL)
1980 Mike Schmidt, Philadelphia (NL)
1981 Ron Cay, Pedro Guerrero,
     Steve Yeager, Los Angeles (NL)
1982 Darrell Porter, St. Louis (NL)
1983 Rick Dempsey, Baltimore (AL)
1984 Alan Trammell, Detroit (AL)
1985 Bret Saberhagen, Kansas City (AL)
1986 Ray Knight, New York (NL)
1987 Frank Viola, Minnesota (AL)
1988 Orel Hershiser, Los Angeles (NL)
1989 Dave Stewart, Oakland (AL)
1990 Jose Rijo, Cincinnati (NL)
1991 Jack Morris, Minnesota (AL)
1992 Pat Borders, Toronto (AL)
1993 Paul Molitor (AL)

LEAGUE CHAMPIONSHIP SERIES MVPS

NATIONAL LEAGUE	YEAR	AMERICAN LEAGUE
Dusty Baker, L.A.	1977	—
Steve Garvey, L.A.	1978	—
Willie Stargell, Phi.	1979	—
Manny Trillo, Phi.	1980	Frank White, K.C.
Burt Hooten, L.A.	1981	Craig Nettles, NY
Darrell Porter, St. L.	1982	Fred Lynn Cal.
Gary Matthews Phi.	1983	Mike Boddicker, Bal.
Steve Garvey S.D.	1984	Kirk Gibson, Del.
Ozzie Smith St. L.	1985	George Brett, K.C.
Mike Scott, Hou.	1986	Marry Barrett Bos.
Jeff Leonard, S.F.	1987	Gary Gaetti Min.
Orel Hershiser, L.A.	1988	Dennis Eckersley Oak.
Will Clark, S.F.	1989	Rickey Henderson, Oak.
*Rob Dibble, Cin. Randy Myers, Cin.	1990	Dave Stewart, Oak.
Steve Avery, Atl.	1991	Kirby Puckett, Min.
John Smoltz, Atl.	1992	Roberto Alomar, Tor.
Curt Schilling, Phi.	1993	Dave Stewart, Tor.

The American League's first LCS MVP award was given in 1980.
* Tie

Here are some other exciting titles for you to order:

BASKETBALL SUPERSTARS ALBUM 1995, by Richard J. Brenner. Includes 16 full-color pages, and mini-bios of the game's top superstars, plus career and all-time stats. 48 pages. ($4.50/$5.50 Can.)

SHAQUILLE O'NEAL * LARRY JOHNSON, by Richard J. Brenner. A dual biography of the two brightest young stars in basketball. 96 pages, 10 pages of photos. ($3.50/$4.50 Can.)

MICHAEL JORDAN * MAGIC JOHNSON by Richard J. Brenner. A dual biography of two of the greatest superstars of all time. 128 pages, 15 dynamite photos. ($3.50/$4.25 Can.)

TROY AIKMAN * STEVE YOUNG, by Richard J. Brenner. A dual biography of the top two quarterbacks in the NFL. 96 pages, 10 pages of photos. ($3.50/$4.50 Can.)

BARRY BONDS * ROBERTO ALOMAR, by Bob Woods. A dual biography of two of the brightest stars in baseball. 96 pages, 10 pages of photos. ($3.50/$4.50 Can.)

MARIO LEMIEUX, by Richard J. Brenner. An exciting biography of one of hockey's all-time greats. 96 pages, 10 pages of photos. ($3.50/$4.50 Can.)

THE WORLD SERIES, THE GREAT CONTESTS, by Richard J. Brenner. The special excitement of the Fall Classic is brought to life through seven of the most thrilling Series ever played, including 1993. 176 pages, including 16 action-packed photos. ($3.50/$4.50 Can.)

THE COMPLETE SUPER BOWL STORY, GAMES I–XXVIII by Richard J. Brenner. The most spectacular moments in Super Bowl history are brought to life, game-by-game. 224 pages, including 16 memorable photos. **($4.00/$5.00 Can.)**

SHAQUILLE O'NEAL, by Richard J. Brenner. An easy-to-read, photo-filled biography especially for younger readers. 32 pages. ($3.25/$4.50 Can.)

MICHAEL JORDAN, by Richard J. Brenner. **An easy-to-read, photo filled biography especially for younger readers. 32 pages. ($3.50/$4.50 Can.)**

WAYNE GRETZKY, by Richard J. Brenner. An easy-to-read, photo-filled biography of hockey's greatest player. 32 pages. Revised edition. ($3.25/$4.50 Can.)

PLEASE SEE NEXT PAGE FOR ORDER FO

ORDER FORM

Please indicate the number of copies of each title that you are ordering.

_____	BASKETBALL SUPERSTARS ALBUM 1995	($4.50/$5.50 Can.)
_____	SHAQUILLE O'NEAL * LARRY JOHNSON	($3.50/$4.50 Can.)
_____	MICHAEL JORDAN * MAGIC JOHNSON	($3.50/$4.25 Can.)
_____	TROY AIKMAN * STEVE YOUNG	($3.50/$4.50 Can.)
_____	BARRY BONDS * ROBERTO ALOMAR	($3.50/$4.50 Can.)
_____	MARIO LEMIEUX	($3.50/$4.50 Can.)
_____	THE WORLD SERIES, THE GREAT CONTESTS	($3.50/$4.50 Can.)
_____	THE COMPLETE SUPER BOWL STORY, GAMES I–XXVIII	($4.00/$5.00 Can.)
_____	SHAQUILLE O'NEAL	($3.25/$4.50 Can.)
_____	MICHAEL JORDAN	($3.50/$4.50 Can.)
_____	WAYNE GRETZKY	($3.25/$4.50 Can.)

Payment must accompany all orders. *All payments must be in U.S. dollars.*

Postage and handling is $1.35 per book up to a maximum of $6.75. ($1.75 to a maximum of $8.75 in Canada.)

TOTAL NUMBER OF BOOKS ORDERED _____

TOTAL COST OF BOOKS $_____

POSTAGE AND HANDLING $_____

TOTAL COST OF ORDER $_____

Please don't forget to enclose a check or money order in U.S. funds only.

Please make checks payable to: EAST END PUBLISHING, Ltd.

54 Alexander Dr.
Syosset, NY 11791

Discounts are available on orders of 25 or more copies. For details, call: (516-364-6383)

_____

Please print neatly.

NAME: _____

ADDRESS: _____

CITY: _____ STATE: _____ ZIP CODE: _____

ASE ALLOW FOUR WEEKS FOR DELIVERY.

Publishing, Ltd., Dept. SB3, 54 Alexander Drive, Syosset, NY